Balíkbayan Boxes
For Better Or For Worse

including

"The Ignorant Immigrant"

"Mga Dilang Pili-Pilipit"

"Doble-Doble"

and other commentaries

Ed Palenque

WingSpan Press

Printed in the United States of America

Published by WingSpan Press, Livermore, CA
www.wingspanpress.com

The WingSpan name, logo and colophon are the
trademarks of WingSpan Publishing.

ISBN 978-1-59594-161-9

First edition 2007

Library of Congress Control Number 2007930439
Available @ ARKIPELAGO Books
1010 Mission Street
San Francisco, CA 94103 USA
www.arkipelagobooks.com

For my two sons

Captain Willy (Alex) and Mister Ray (Ray)

There's a whole big world out there......

CONTENTS

PREFACE

Ask any overseas Filipino and they will know the concept and stimulus behind Balikbayan boxes. The term Balikbayan literally means "return to home country." Balikbayan boxes are the boxes that many expatriate Filipinos fill with goodies from their adopted country and send to their relatives and friends in the old country. There is even an offshoot of this idea that allows customers to specify what items to include in a Balikbayan box. Christmas boxes can be filled – for an extra fee of course – with yummy and nostalgic *queso de bola* (ball of acrid cheese) and other traditional Christmas food items.

My argument in "Balikbayan Boxes – For Better or For Worse" is that sending the boxes is not a good thing because it makes our relatives and friends overly dependent upon us, and it reinforces the corruption in various government offices, not the least of all the customs bureau. My original title was "Balikbayan Boxes are Evil," but since I've somewhat mellowed with age, I decided to change the title and give readers a chance to decide for themselves.

Elsewhere in these pages...

"This Likely Won't Skip A Generation" is a small collection of admonitions from our elders. Some do make sense while others are outright nonsense. As to which ones are which, you be the judge.

"Chinese New Year" explores various aspects of Spring festival. Many of my observations are from first-hand experience when I lived in the People's Republic part of the last two decades of the last century; many of the beliefs about which I write have been incorporated into Filipino tradition.

"Keynote Speech by Senator Juan Flavier, MD" is my humble recollection of remarks that the Senator made at a UP Alumni Association–America reunion held in Houston, Texas. Senator Flavier was an occasional speaker at various student functions at the University of the Philippines in the early 70s. His hard-hitting stories mixed humor and a moral and made his few visits to the university memorable – even after all these years.

I attended the wedding of my wife's cousin, and "A Sniper at the Memphis Wedding" is the disorderly outcome. It is guaranteed to clutter your mind with curious and sometimes trivial matters. By contrast, "Deep in the Heart of Tejas" was conceived during a visit to Texas and is a partial atonement for my initial total lack of emotion about the Alamo, LBJ and other historical people and circumstances. Shame on me. Just a little research revealed many spectacular events that occurred in the areas of San Antonio and Austin.

The Filipino language – its constructs, sounds and peculiarities – is the subject of four essays: "Use the Right Word; Put the Accent on the Correct Sylláble," "Doble – Doble" (Double-Double), "Mga Dilang Pilí-pilipít" (Inter-twisted Tongues), and "Different Words." No philosophical musings or political diatribes here. I only hope you have as much fun reading them as I had writing them. Also, just because many things have been repeated many times over does not mean I can't state them again. The result is "You May Be Getting Old When..."

I won't ever deny it. The USA, in my opinion, is one of the most socialist states in the world. "The Ignorant Immigrant" lists just a few of the things my feeble mind observes and tries to comprehend without much success. I plead with the reader to help me resolve these matters that burden my perplexed brain.

"Traditional Filipino Last Names" is a listing of some names the writer recalls from way back. This is a short list. There are surely many other traditional names out there. The reason this is significant is that many last names in the Philippines are Spanish (e.g. Reyes) or Chinese (e.g. Lee).

"Cheating Las Vegas" reveals some ways people attempt to cheat the superpower corporations that run the spectacle in the desert meadows. I've often wondered if this seemingly irresistible attraction to gambling is more pronounced in Filipinos than in other peoples, but I doubt it. I've seen many serious players in Macau, and I hear the casinos of Monte Carlo are constantly filled with players of all nationalities. And here in the US the so-called riverboat casinos are not empty either.

Don't try any of the cheating techniques, though. I don't want to be sued.

In "Don't Mistake Schooling for Education" I insist that there is a distinct difference between going to school and what I call education. It is well known that Filipinos stress going to school and earning degrees and becoming so-called professionals. Even today, in small barrios, one sees signs on houses proclaiming "Maria C. Reyes – Lady CPA" or "Jose R. Gonzales – Civil Engineer." This article hopes to remind young people that to enhance their schooling, they need to acquire many other skills like teamwork, networking, leadership, math skills, computer savvy, public speaking, good grooming, negotiating and so on.

In "Copy Watches at a Beer House in Mandaluyong," the owner of a beerhouse entices the writer to purchase an Omega Rolex knockoff watch. Do I yield to the temptation? Do I refuse on moral grounds? Read on!

Finally...
Someone said that writing a book is a great indulgence of the ego, whatever that means. My first objective is to offer a style of thinking about social issues. We do not have to accept the current structure as it is. We can propose changes and act differently. I hope my commentaries on social issues stir something inside the reader's heart. My second objective is to document in a non-academic, plain and unpretentious way some of the quaint aspects of dozens of Filipino words. Many people take these distinctive characteristics for granted but I hope they will find my articles on the subject totally entertaining.

Finally, I sure hope this work becomes a commercial success. I therefore shamelessly request that the reader promote this work among his or her friends, Filipinos or not. Or if you don't have any friends, please recommend this book to any people you know. Your kind act will surely be rewarded in the future.

My editor Judy Clement Wall of JCW Editing was extraordinary for her grammar and syntax adjustments on the original manuscript. My excuse was there were no advanced English composition courses required for my industrial engineering degree. She dared confront me, with great professional aplomb and pitiless assertiveness, about my many flawed arguments, vague supporting statements and unclear conclusions. These confrontations by email I believe improved my propositions and presented my arguments on a more solid basis, especially on some controversial matters.

My bruised self-esteem from these sparring sessions made me want to blame the editor for any other errors that remain in this work; however, I was informed by the publisher that it is customary to thank the editor nevertheless.

So, I profusely thank the editor for all her effort. There. And I stingily accept all responsibility for any other remaining errors, defects, and inconsistencies in argument or thought. There!

Maraming salamat pò. *Thank you very much.*

BALÍKBAYAN BOXES:
FOR BETTER OR FOR WORSE

This I believe: sending Balikbayan Boxes (BBs) is evil. It reinforces the senders' misplaced, self-imposed duty to help their relatives. It also strengthens the receivers' *bahala na* (let it happen, whatever) attitude and dependence on others, thus further reducing self-reliance – a truly vicious cycle. Receivers of BBs also lose sight of probably the biggest reason for their perennial dependence on others: the failure of the government to provide opportunity to the common *tao* (person) by eliminating corruption and removing economic obstacles to development.

BBs are a concise manifestation of a distorted sense of Filipino clannish behavior, *pasikat* (a form of boasting, ostentatiously subtle, if there is such a thing), materialism and sentimentality. I once overheard a young employee at a thrift store in Las Vegas. She was telling a friend, "*Hindi ako nanono-od ng mga show kasi mahal. Nagpapadala nalang ako ng pera sa kapatid ko.*"

("I don't watch any shows because tickets are expensive. I just send the money to my siblings.") If I were impolite I would have asked her, *"Bakit pa?"* ("Why?")

I am not against helping people, but I think that any help should be in the form of moving people toward self-reliance – not in perpetuating an everlasting reliance on others. Sad to say, most of the help BBs provide are in the form of "as it was in the beginning, is now and forever, world without end…" You know the rest.

For a visiting balikbayan, it would be infinitely shameful not to bring BBs filled with name brand stuff for siblings, parents, cousins, old classmates, etc. As for me, if I visit the Philippines and relatives complain about my bringing nothing fancy, I would say, "Tough!"

Note that a typical BB contains the following items: toothpaste, pillowcases, Ivory bath soap, corned beef, bath towels, chocolate, canned fruit, pasta, pasta sauce, Spam, baseball caps, shampoo, toys, NBA basketball jerseys, bed sheets, T-shirts, peanut butter, movie videos, sports shoes, electronic gadgets. All of that, and I'm sure I've missed a lot. Other items that people send are hand-me-down or bargain clothing. The cost of sending the box can often be much higher than the value of the items it contains.

Furthermore, since a large part of the freight cost is used to grease the Customs people, senders are in effect reinforcing corruption to send their *kawawang* (pitiful) relatives various items. All this is done in the name of *awà* (pity), *pakikisama* (getting along with others), clannishness, *pasíkat* (ostentatious pride), and sentimentality. I'm not complaining about the senders' wasting their money – it's their money, not mine. What bothers me is that senders do not realize, or disregard the fact, that their act further encourages corrupt officials to continue their larceny.

BB senders also unwittingly make their relatives less self-reliant. I asked one sender why she didn't just send money. I proposed that sending money would probably be less expensive and less troublesome than accumulating items for BBs. The answer I got was that their relatives would probably spend the money on non-essential things. Wow! So I guess we have to forever impose discipline on our undisciplined relatives – in the hope that they will someday learn to be disciplined? With this approach, I can't see how that will ever happen.

BBs reduce the receivers' antagonism against a perpetually corrupt political system. In fact, the requisite corruption at the Customs Bureau for the efficient inflow of BBs is totally overlooked. Ask anyone if it is possible to send legitimate commercial cargo into (or out of) the Philippines without grease money. We all know the answer. I wonder if anybody ever wonders how the obviously valuable items in BBs are able to get into the country without much trouble. If there is actually a legitimate fee for a flat customs tax, it is not stated anywhere on the receipt. The fee to ship a BB from your home to its final destination is $65, and that's all there is to it. Some people may say that we should not mess with the price of $65, which is obviously what the open market will bear. I wonder how that breaks down. How much is for the person who picks up, how much for the shipping line, how much for the Customs officials, etc.

But isn't it wrong that a few entrenched bureaucrats in the Customs bureau are getting rich at the expense of others? I understand that this deranged complaint of mine is objectionable, given the long-prevailing mentality that government corruption is expected. Alas, my idea that government employees should not get rich at the expense of others is totally out of line with an ingrained social concept that glorifies the rich (even when they are corrupt).

I came across an article on the internet reporting that BBs are insured for about $250 each. Let's say that's the approximate value of items in the box, which sounds about right. Another story states that BBs come into the country in containers of either 150 boxes or 300 boxes. At $250 per box, we can estimate the value of goods at $37,500 for a container of 150, and $75,000 for a container of 300. The Philippines receives 30 such containers a day. If we assume the 30 containers are divided equally between the two sizes, then the Philippines is getting about $1.65 million per day, or $50 million per month. The article concludes with righteous anger, "*sa ikauunlad ng bayan – dollar ang kailangan*" ("for the progress of the nation, dollars are needed"). I beg to disagree.

The article disregards the fact that dollars alone cannot ensure more opportunity for the common *tao* – especially with an entrenched corrupt political structure. If I read the statistics right, almost a third of the Philippines' annual revenue in recent years (currently about $16 billion), comes from overseas inbound remittances – which does not include money that is hand-carried. That has not made the country richer and more prosperous, even after so many years. So how then can more dollars by itself make it rich now?

Let's not kid ourselves; more dollars will make only a small segment of the population richer. The *common tao* (the masses) will remain as they have been in the past.

As it was in the beginning, is now and forever.

You know the rest.

This Likely Won't Skip A Generation

If I stop for a moment and think about the sources of my knowledge and wisdom, I find that a lot of it has been handed down to me from the past, from parents, siblings, cousins, uncles, aunts, *lolos* and *lolas* (grandfathers and grandmothers), friends, enemies. And, as is usual for most things passed from one generation to the next, some of what I've been given is good, while some is of dubious value or even downright nonsense.

A big part of who I am now, how I behave, what I believe, was formed through interaction with my parents (or maybe a grandparent or aunt). Looking back, I realize that a lot of their admonitions and scolding had to do with making me do what they wanted.

There was only a very brief period of time when they could physically handle me. When I was a baby, a toddler, they could move me from one place to another, say, from the bed to the crib or playpen. As a baby, I could not escape because of my physical limitations. After a couple of years, I became physically bigger and had a mind of my own. I grew assertive and ready to sulk and pout and harass my parents at the slightest provocation.

At about that time, my parents turned to what was familiar, what they had endured from their parents when they were little. They resorted to the use of verbal tools to try to subjugate me. These verbal tools were learned from their parents. I am sure we all had our share of these verbal assaults from our parents and other older people.

Here are just some words of wisdom and terror techniques I remember.

✓ *"Makukubà ka."* (**"You will become a hunchback."**) **What will happen to you if you don't maintain a good posture**

✓ *"Makuha ka sa tingin."* (**"Please heed my glare."**) **More than words can say.**

✓ *"Ubusin mo ang pagkain mo! Marami ibáng tao nagugutom."* (**"Finish up your food. Many other people are starving."**) **Save the world.**

✓ *"Ano ka, sinu-swerte?"* (**"You would be so lucky?"** **– delivered in a sarcastic tone.) Don't ever try to aim for the stars.**

✓ *"Tingnan mo ang kapatid mo - - -"* (**"Look, see your sibling..."**) **Move away from individuality, stop being yourself.**

✓ *"Pagbutíhin mo."* (**"Please do your best."**) **I know you want to fail, but please do your best.**

Below is a creative series from among the many emails I receive from various sources. *"Hinding-hindî ko makakalimutan ang mga mumuntí ngunit ginintuáng butil ng payo na nakuha ko sa aking mga magulang."* (**"I can't ever forget the many tiny but golden bits of advice that I received from my parents."**)

1. *Si Inay, tinuruan niya ako* (**My mother taught me**) **how to appreciate a job well done**: *"Kung kayong dalawá ay magpapatayan, doon kayó sa labás! Mga leche kayó, kalilinis ko lang ng bahay!"* (**"If you two are fighting to the death, do it outdoors. You are pests, I have just cleaned the house!"**)

2. *Natuto ako ng* **religion** *kay Itay.* (**I learned religion from my father.**) *"Kapag yang mantsa di natanggal sa carpet, magdasal ka na!"* (**"If the stain on the carpet won't come off, you'd better start praying!"**)

3. *Kay Inay ako natuto ng* **logic.** (**From my mother, I learned logic.**) *"Kaya ganyan, dahil sinabi ko."* (**"The reason it's that way is I said so."**)

4. *At kay Inay pa rin ako natuto ng* **more logic.** (**And from my mother I learned more logic.**) *"Kapag ikáw ay nalaglág diyán sa bubóng, ako lang mag-isáng manonood ng sine!"* (**"If you fall off that roof, I shall be going to the movies by myself!"**)

5. *Si Inay din ang nagturò sa akin kung ano ang ibig sabihin ng* irony. **(It was also my mother who taught me the meaning of irony.)** *"Sigé ngumalngal ka pa at bibigyan talagá kita ng iiyakan mo!"* **("Go ahead and continue crying – and I will give you a reason to really cry!")**

6. *Si Inay ang nagpaliwanag sa akin kung ano ang* **contortionism. (My mother was the one who explained the meaning of contortionism.)** *"Tingnan mo nga yang dumí sa likód ng leég mo, tignán mo!!"* **("Just look at the dirt behind your neck! Look at it !")**

7. *Si Itay ang nagpaliwanag sa akin kung anong ibig sabihin ng* **stamina.(It was my father who explained to me the meaning of stamina.)** *"Huwág kang tatayô diyan hangga't di mo natatapos yang lahat ng pagkain mo!"* **("Don't get up until you've finished eating all of your food!")**

8. *At si Inay ang nagturò sa amin kung ano ang* **weather. (My mother taught us about weather.)** *"Lintek talagá kayó, anó ba itóng kuwarto nyong magkapatid, parang dinaanan ng bagyó!"* **("You're all messed up, your room looks like one damaged by a hurricane!")**

9. *Ganito ang paliwanag sa akin ni Inay tungkol sa* **circle of life: (This is how my mother explained the circle of life.)** *"Malandî kang batà ka, iniluwál kita sa mundóng ito, maari rin kitáng alisín sa mundong ito."* **("You petulant child. I brought you into this world. And I can very well remove you from this world.")**

10. *Kay Itay ako natuto kung ano ang* **behavior modification. (I learned behavior modification from my father.)** *"Tumigil ka nga diyan! Huwag kang mag-inarte na parang Nanay mo!"* (**"Stop behaving that way. Don't be like your mother!"**)

11. *Si Inay naman ang nagturo kung anong ibig sabihin ng* **genetics. (My mother explained the meaning of genetics.)** *"Nagmana ka ngang talagá sa ama mong walanghiyâ!"* (**"You really take after your shameless father!"**)

12. *Si Inay naman ang nagpaliwanag sa amin kung anong ibig sabihin ng* **envy. (My mother explained the meaning of envy)** *"Maraming mga batang ulilà sa magulang, di ba kayo nagpapasalamat at mayroon kayong magulang na tulad namin?"* (**"There are many orphaned children; should you not be grateful you have parents like us?"**)

13. *Si Itay naman ang nagturò sa akin ng* **anticipation. (My father taught me anticipation.)** *"Sige kang batà ka, hintayin mong makarating tayo sa ; bahay!"* (**"Go ahead, kid; just wait till we get home."**)

14. *At si Itay pa rin ang nagturò kay Kuya kung anong ibig sabihin ng* **receiving. (Father also taught my big brother the meaning of receiving.)** *"Uupakan kita pagdating natin sa bahay!"* (**"I will beat you up when we get home!"**)

15. *Si Inay naman ang nagturò sa akin kung ano ang* **humor. (Mother taught me what humor was.)** *"Kapag naputol yang mga paa mo ng pinaglalaruan mong lawnmower, huwag na huwag kang tatakbo*

sa akin at lulumpuhín kita!" (**"If your foot gets cut off playing with the lawnmower, don't ever come running to me because I will make you a cripple."**)

16. *At ang pinakamahalagá sa lahat, natutúnan ko kina Inay at Itay kung ano ang* **justice**. (**And most priceless of all, I learned from mother and father the meaning of justice.**) *"Sang araw magkakaroon ka rin ng anak, tiyak maging katulad mo at magiging pasakit din sa ulo!"* (**"Someday you will also have children, surely just like you, and they too will be a big headache!"**)

And finally, a word for some parents who may themselves occasionally behave like they are insane. I define insanity as not changing the way you do things, yet expecting to get different results. If you keep doing or saying something to your children, and it does not achieve the desired results, you should think of *other* means to achieve the desired results, other newer words to say and possibly other more innovative acts of terrorism. That is the only way to maintain sanity, yours and your kids'.

Meantime, the wisdom of the ages keeps getting passed on. It just keeps rolling along.

This likely won't skip a generation.

CHINESE NEW YEAR

The history goes as follows: in the old days, the reigning emperor established the start of the Chinese New Year by imperial decree. Nowadays, celebrations are based on Emperor Han Wu Di's almanac. Han Wu Di held power from 156-87 B.C. The almanac specifies the first day of the first month of the lunar year as the start of Chinese New Year or *Chun Jie* (Spring Festival) the term used in China. It is undoubtedly the most important holiday for almost a quarter of the world's population. It is a fixed date on the Chinese Lunar Calendar but always falls between January 20 and February 19 in the Gregorian calendar.

In China, the lunar New Year occurs 16 hours ahead of U.S. Pacific Standard Time. To make sure you celebrate on the right date, use a Chinese calendar if you have one. In the U.S., most commercially available (non-Chinese) calendars indicate Chinese New Year. We definitely don't want people performing lion dances or lighting firecrackers or frying *tikoy* (a type of sweet cake) at the wrong time. That would be improper, if not downright unlucky.

You may be wondering about "Gong He Xing Xi" and "Gong He Fat Choy." Not to worry. They are both New Year greetings. If the reader is more familiar with the latter, it is probably because that Cantonese expression is more pervasive. Recent estimates indicate that about 80 percent of all Chinese in the US trace their origins to Canton (Guangzhou) province. Hope that settles that.

Every year, the Spring festival highlights one of twelve animals. According to legend, the animal of your birth year "is the animal that hides in your soul." All Chinese souvenir shops have some chart that shows the animal associated with your birth year. These charts also show your typical personality attributes and the people of other animal years with whom you are likely to be compatible or incompatible.

My birth year is the year of the dragon, supposedly a lucky year. It is said that people born in the year of the dragon are "destined for greatness." Alas, they did not say what form the greatness would take. But I'm ever so patient.

These are the equivalent years of the dragon using our familiar calendar: 1904, 1916, 1928, 1940, 1952, 1964, 1976, 1988, 2000, 2012, 2024. So the oldest I could possibly be is 102 years old !

Other words used to describe people born in the year of the dragon are: charismatic, magnanimous, self-assured, artistic, intuitive, and very lucky. At the same time, dragons are often impulsive, irritable, eccentric, proud and stubborn. A probable reason for these mixed characteristics is that the dragon in old tales has always been described as enchanting, stirring human emotion in many ways.

Hong Bao

New year traditions include giving children, unmarried friends, and servants money (crisp dollar bills) in little red packets called *hong-bao* – *hong* meaning red and *bao* meaning packet. These red packets, also called *lai-see*, bring good fortune. In olden days, heads of households also took time to serve meals and beverages to their servants and helpers. It is indeed a rare occasion when masters are shouted orders by their servants, "More food here! More wine! Make it quick!"

Firecrackers and Spring Couplets

It is an old custom to light firecrackers to scare away the legendary beast, Nian, that, according to old stories, preyed on people on new year's eve. It is believed that Nian is afraid of firecrackers and the color red. It's amusing that the word *nian* means year. A related tradition is putting up couplets in doorways. These are elegant characters written on red paper and pasted onto both sides of doorways. These couplets welcome the New Year and drive away evil spirits. The themes of these short poems are happiness, good fortune, longevity, and wealth. Ready-printed couplets are available at all local Asian stores – although many people still make these themselves. Paste one vertical couplet on each side of the doorway and a horizontal one on top. Be sure you put them on their proper side and make certain the top one matches the subject of the side couplets. If you don't read Chinese characters, ask the Chinese people at the store to help you find verses that sound good to you.

Some people, this writer included, also put an upside-down *"Fu"* character in the middle of their front door, around eye level. *Fu* is variously defined as good blessing, fortune or luck. The idea is for the gods to see the character upright when viewed from the heavens. Another interpretation is that the Chinese word for upside-down has the same sound as the word for "arrival."

In Chinatown, San Francisco, aside from the traditional Chinese festivities, there are more modern celebrations that take place. There is a Miss Chinatown beauty pageant and a coronation grand ball. Chambers of commerce usually organize these events while various businesses sponsor different parts of the festivities. There is also a market fair and often a carnival fair, as well as a 5K or 10K Run/Walk fundraising event.

The traditional lion dance is believed to ward off evil demons. Each lion is supposed to have two dancers, one to control the head and the other to rein-in the back end. Lions, while not indigenous to China, are held to be good omens. Sculptured statues of lions, some with a raised right paw, are frequently seen guarding entrances to private and government buildings and temples. The traditional gate to the San Francisco Chinatown on the corner of Grant and Bush St has these lions.

Do You Owe People Money?
Here's a special note if you owe people money. Spring Festival is one of three auspicious days when accounts have to be settled. (The other two are the Dragon Boat Festival and the Thanksgiving Harvest Festival.) So if any of you readers owe anyone money, the time to settle up is now – before dawn of the first day of spring! My research did not point to specific penalties for non-compliance, but it did say that good luck will come to you if you pay

up in time. If some people owe you money, you should <u>now</u> gear up your collection process. I imagine if you owe people money, you should expect to receive demands for payment soon. If you cannot or don't want to pay, you may want to try the ingenious technique described below.

There is an old story about a debtor who was not inclined to repay his debt. He got especially concerned as the Spring Festival approached, so he devised a technique to have the debt forgiven. Every time he would meet the lender on the street, he would bow profusely, stretch his arms wide, get on his knees and in a loud voice ask for forgiveness for his *delay* in repaying the debt. He would continue in his loud, dramatic voice, listing his problems – slow business, a sick child, etc. – and again seeking forgiveness for his *delay* in repaying the debt. Not surprisingly, this dramatic ploy in a public street greatly embarrassed the lender. And guess what, the lender eventually forgave the debt. Don't try this at home.

OTHER TRADITIONS

It is a traditional practice during Chinese New Year celebration for people to buy presents, decorations, special foods and new clothing. The weeks leading up to spring festival create madhouses at large department stores in China, much like Costco or Wal-Mart or Target between Thanksgiving and Christmas here in the US. In the Sacramento area, the shopping frenzy and excitement around Spring Festival is centered on Asian markets.

In China, millions of travelers take vacation days around New Year to return home for family reunions. All the railroad stations become jam-packed. It is said that the Beijing train station (*huoche zhan*) alone regularly handles over 300,000 people daily; it is not unusual for that figure to more than quadruple around the spring festival. Not surprising, the train stations are usually deserted on the New Year's Day itself - even though trains still run on schedule.

Some years back, a news article reported that China has instituted measures to prevent the spread of sickness (SARS included) during the Spring Festival travel period. It said that travelers with coughs and temperatures between 37.5 and 38 degrees C (about 100.5 F) will not be allowed to board trains. I can only imagine the delay this screening will create for the estimated 1.89 billion journeys expected around this major holiday. Then again, I think that even the Chinese bureaucracy will most probably do only random checks to avoid mass turmoil.

HOUSE CLEANING

Traditionally, families give their homes a thorough cleaning before spring festival. I wonder if this is the reason we see a lot of flyers for home cleaning on our front doors right about this time? Cleaning sweeps away bad luck and makes the house ready for good luck to cross the threshold. After the cleaning, all sweeping paraphernalia must be put away on New Year's Eve - so good luck cannot be swept away. Be sure you follow these instructions closely.

OTHER TRADITIONS FOR LUCK

It is a lucky sign to see or hear songbirds or red-colored birds or swallows. Do not use knives or scissors on New Year's Day as this may cut off fortune. Red clothing is preferred during this festive occasion. Red is considered a bright, happy color, sure to bring the wearer a sunny and bright future. It is believed that good appearance, polite attitude and pleasant behavior during New Year's day sets the tone for the rest of the year.

To ensure long life and good luck, eat fish. Avoid red meat on New Year's Day. Eating red dates can induce great wealth. Eating melon seeds is said to point to many healthy children. Oranges and tangerines also symbolize wealth and good fortune. When you visit relatives during the spring festival period, you should always bring bags with oranges and tangerines. The tangerines should have stems with leaves on them.

Some people keep open all the windows and doors in the house to facilitate the departure of the old year though I would be hesitant if the weather is cold – as is usually the case in northern China during Spring Festival. (Beijing is around +39 deg latitude while Canton is almost tropical at around +22 deg latitude.) Others keep the lights in the house on the whole night. And of course, there are the almost mandatory firecrackers and other fireworks at midnight. Some families place coins of various denominations on windowsills all around the house, in the belief that the coins will attract wealth into the house during the new year.

TABOOS

There are many other beliefs that trace their origin to old stories. Many people abstain from meat on New Year's day confident that they will partake of many happy events during the year. Also, be careful not to serve or eat any food from a chipped or cracked vessel, plate, cup, bowl or whatever.

Others do not wash their hair on this day because they might wash away good luck. This is interpreted many ways;

some people say this admonition applies to shaving, others say it applies to having a haircut. It is a common belief that if you cry during this day, you will be crying throughout the year, so parents really spoil little children on this day – we don't want them to cry or complain about anything on New Year's Day. This belief has been expanded to mean – whatever you are doing on New Year's Day, you'll be doing for the rest of the year. So be careful not to be caught sleeping or fighting or drunk or angry at the stroke of midnight!

The Spring Festival celebrations wind up on the 15th day of the first lunar month with the Lantern Festival. Young men highlight the parade with a dragon dance and people carry lanterns to the parade. Keep in mind that the Chinese dragon is not the same as its medieval incarnation which represents terror and destruction. The Chinese dragon is described as the "genius of strength and goodness." It brings good fortune and luck. It is the symbol of vigilance and safeguard. People born in the year of the dragon are destined for greatness. The dragon is the chief of all scaly reptiles. An ancient story relates that the dragon, after a period of hibernation, emerges in the spring, thus announcing by it's awakening the return of nature's energies. The dragon is made up of parts of nine animals. It has the head of a camel, horns of a deer, eyes of a rabbit, ears of a cow, neck of snake, belly of a frog, scales of carp, claws of a hawk and the palm of a tiger.

The next 12 years' occurrence of Spring Festival is shown below with the Chinese year, animal, and our regular Gregorian calendar date.

4705 Boar   February 18, 2007
4706 Rat   February 7, 2008
4707 Ox   January 26, 2009
4708 Tiger   February 10, 2010
4709 Hare/Rabbit February 3, 2011
4710 Dragon   January 23, 2012
4711 Snake   February 10, 2013
4712 Horse   January 31, 2014
4713 Ram/Sheep   February 19, 2015
4714 Monkey   February 8, 2016
4715 Rooster   January 28, 2017
4716 Dog   February 16, 2018

KEYNOTE SPEECH BY UP ALUMNUS SENATOR JUAN FLAVIER, MD

This whole episode started when, seemingly out of nowhere, I received an email from Joe, a fraternity brother from the engineering college at the University of the Philippines in the early 70s. He had settled in the Los Angeles area where other fraternity brothers live. Joe reported that a group of brothers in the Houston area were sponsoring a show featuring the UP Concert Chorus as part of the university-wide alumni reunion in that city. The keynote speaker would be Senator Juan Flavier, MD, a distinguished alumnus of the university, and an elected senator.

I remember Dr. Juan Flavier very well from the various talks he gave at the university during our time. He had always been a rural doctor. I specifically recall a technique he used for cooling a patient in the *barrio*. He said there was no ice in many rural areas so they would use the inner part of the trunks of banana trees. (He has published the following books: *Doctor to the Barrios, Parables of the Barrios, My Friends in the Barrios, Back to the Barrios*. His columns are still widely published in various Filipino community newspapers.

Aside from the many practical things Dr Flavier would relate, he would invariably tell us funny stories with moral lessons. I recall one story in particular, intended to encourage volunteerism for a good cause. I believe it was at first floor auditorium at the old College of Arts and Sciences in Diliman in the raucous early 70s.

He narrated a story of Berto and his teenage buddies. They were walking over a bridge when they heard cries for help coming from the river below. They looked down and there was a person waving his arms, obviously in distress. Everyone got excited but no one seemed to know what to do. A couple of seconds later Berto was in the river pulling the person out, shouts of hurrah all around. The parents of the kids asked Berto why he quickly decided to help the person in distress. Berto admitted that he was hesitant to help, but when he was *pushed* by someone into the river, he had no choice.

Dr Flavier told the alumni group in Houston this same story of Berto. This story, emphasizing the giving of one's self for others, ended his brief talk to a standing ovation. With humor, he had reminded us of the extreme necessity and enduring benefit of helping in any way we could our university back in the old country.

But wait, there's more. Before this story of Berto, Senator Flavier began his talk with these remarks at the Houston alumni reunion. Needless to say, it was non-stop laughing and whistling and yelling. Be warned, this is just my humble recollection. I have taken the liberty of paraphrasing where I do not recall his exact words:

Thank you for the kind introduction. All please be seated right now. Please! I don't want anyone to be taller than me. (Note: Sen Juan Flavier claims to be 4 ft 11 in.).

As you know, I can't accept all invitations to speak because if I did, I would be speaking five times a day and would never be able to do anything else. But I accepted your kind invitation to speak in large part because UP is very close to my heart. (Loud applause)

Also, the people on the convention committee were very, very smart... Actually, they did not invite me... They invited my wife... and who am I to say anything ? (Loud laughter.)

Like many fellow alumni, I am a Canadian (*ka na diyan*). My wife continually tells me – "*maglinis ka na diyan*" (you clean up right now) and "*magligpit ka na diyan*" (you set things aside right now) and "*magluto ka na diyan*" (you do the cooking right now) and "*maghugas ka na diyan*" (you do the dishes right now)

Also, this is a weekend and I have time to fly back home to the Philippines. I do not want to be absent for any session of the Philippine Senate. I have had perfect attendance for the past 8 years. (Loud applause)

I remember my mother said, "*Hindi bale kung bobo ka. Basta perfect attendance ka, ma-aawa ang teacher at siguradong ipapasá ka.*" ("It matters not that you are not bright, with perfect attendance the teacher will pity you and will give you a passing grade.")

That is true. I passed.

Dr. --- over there was my seatmate at UP. During exams, I copied from him...
That is why I almost failed. (Loud laughter.)

In the (Philippine) Senate, I am known as Juan "the short." Another Juan in the Senate boasts he is Juan "the tall." *Kasi daw 6' 2" – daw.* But that is actually 6 ft (vertical dimension hand motion) and 2 inches (below waistline frontal horizontal dimension hand motion). I am Juan "the short" at 4 ft 11 inches (no hand motion).

The press made a big story of this. One reporter even called my wife to verify the dimension in question. My wife replied, "Well, the senator is entitled to his own optical illusion."

A SNIPER AT THE
MEMPHIS WEDDING

I attended a wedding in Memphis recently. The ceremony, held at the Cathedral of the Immaculate Conception on tree-lined Central Avenue near downtown Memphis, ended around 2 p.m. on a sunny Saturday. The mandatory picture-taking sessions followed. I figured that would take at least another hour. Since I was not a member of the official wedding entourage, I decided to go to the Wal-Mart super-center on Hwy 46, east of Germantown Blvd. It would be cool to quickly order 1-hour prints of the candid pictures I had taken and present them to the couple as a little add-on gift.

It is amazing how most wedding photographers take so long, usually several weeks, to make pictures available. Don't they know they would sell more if the pictures were available within a few days? As with most extravagant affairs, the excitement quickly diminishes with the passage of time. Also, the couple invariably feels they spent too much on the wedding and therefore will not be inclined to order many copies.

Most of the wedding guests were from Oxnard, CA, or Memphis, TN. The couple was originally from Oxnard and the bride's parents moved to Memphis. The groom, Dominic, my wife's cousin, followed his heart. So there. Other relatives were from New York, San Diego, and Sacramento.

The rehearsal dinner the Friday night before had a nice bit of political discussion about Mr. Bush and Mr. Kerry – remember them? Not unexpectedly, the people from New York were die-hard liberals who preferred a nanny government. Others – reflecting the popular vote – wanted less government intrusion into people's lives. We made sure knives and other sharp objects were taken off the dining table during the political discussions.

Especially because some uncles were imbibing adult beverages.

Memphis is the eighteenth-largest city in the US, a large town of over 650,000 on the Mississippi River. It was named after the ancient Egyptian capital on the river Nile. Nashville lies to the east, St Louis Missouri to the north. Between Memphis and St Louis is Cape Girardeau, hometown of Rush Limbaugh. Tupelo, Mississippi where Elvis was born, is about two hours southeast of Memphis.

The first Holiday Inn opened in Memphis – in 1952. Fed-Ex was founded in the late 70s and Memphis is its headquarters. Memphis touts itself as America's Distribution Center, with overnight road or railway connections to over 150 metropolitan markets covering over 65 percent of the US population

Even so, if you think Fed-Ex is the largest employer in Memphis, you're dead wrong. You know it's the, ahem, government! Ha, I got you. Fed-Ex only has 28,000 or about 23 percent of jobs, while the government agencies based in Memphis (federal, city, county, state, university) cover about 56,000 employees, or about 46 percent of jobs!

Famous people with affiliations in Memphis include the best-selling author John Grisham. Two movies adapted from his novels, *The Firm* and *The Client*, were shot in Memphis. Alex Haley, author of *Roots*, was born in Henning 60 miles away.

I visited the standard tourist sites...

The Peabody Hotel – a 12-story refurbished old Spanish-style hunting lodge in the heart of downtown. The elegant main lobby, though relatively small and a bit crowded, is said to be the place to see and be seen. I'm from out of state so it didn't matter that much to me. The function room where the wedding reception was held was beautifully ornate but seemed to show its age. I wonder if that's why they kept the lights dim all through the night.

Beale Street – a dense 3-block cluster of jazz clubs, bars, restaurants and gift shops, promoted as the birthplace of many jazz greats. By the way, drinking in public is allowed within this two- to three-block area only. To make sure it was clear when I was there, police cars were parked on the corners and several police officers were on duty. The unspoken message: Drink all you want but please behave.

FedEx Forum – the new home of the Memphis Grizzlies NBA team. I didn't get to visit the Pyramid or the Coliseum.

The Houston Rockets were playing the Grizzlies on the Friday night I arrived, but I wasn't inclined to deal with scalpers so I decided against it.

Graceland – the mansion bought from the Moore family by Elvis Presley in 1957 for his mother Gladys. Sadly, Gladys Presley died in 1958. Elvis reportedly paid $100,000 for 13+ acres and the mansion at a time when the average annual household income was about $1,250. The mansion itself is small; I estimate it's just 4,000 square feet. With well over 700,000 visitors a year, Graceland has the distinction of being the second most visited home in the US – after the White House.

Separate structures in the back include the garage, which was eventually converted into business offices for Vernon Presley, his father. There is a so-called trophy room which contains Elvis' gold (and other) records. A short walk behind the trophy room is a racquetball court that has been converted into a display room for Elvis' various show costumes and yet more gold records. Elvis sold more than billion records worldwide. In the US alone, he had eighteen number one records, forty Top-10 Hits and 114 Top-40 Singles. Wow.

Elvis' 1973 TV special, "Elvis – Aloha from Hawaii, via Satellite," was viewed by over 1.5 billion people in over forty countries. It was reportedly seen in more US homes than was man's first walk on the moon just a few years earlier.

The thing I didn't like about the souvenir shops inside the Graceland area were the prices. The only item I purchased was a glossy 8" x 11" Graceland Official guidebook, which was a very reasonable $10. Everything else - the T-shirts, sweatshirts, hats, cups were priced too steeply. With all due respect, that's probably why

the Elvis estate still generates over $40 million annually
– even thirty years after his death in 1976!

Elvis' final resting place, along with other family
members, is on the south side of the mansion in what
is called the Garden of Meditation. The garden is always
full of flowers, posters, ribbons, etc., from all over the
world. Graceland policy is to accept all types of tributes
to Elvis for the garden – fresh, plastic, paper, posters,
ceramic, whatever. There are over five hundred active fan
clubs operating all over the world – more than for any
other celebrity, living or dead. I find this really amazing.

Tunica, Mississippi – about thirty miles south of
the Memphis city border. If you've been to Reno or Las
Vegas, Tunica will disappoint you - if only because the
casino hotels are at least a couple of miles from each
other – not the usual tight, side-by-side setting in Vegas
or Reno. Tunica has Grand, Bally's, Sheraton, Sam's
Town, Hollywood, Harrah's and a few little ones. I stuck
by tradition, contributing, of my own free will, $40 to
each of the casinos I visited. Don't try this at home.

Corky's BBQ – It seems that Memphis has BBQ places
on every street corner. Like Starbucks in Seattle, I guess.
Corky's original location is at 5259 Poplar Avenue. There
is a branch in Germantown and an outlet at the Memphis
International Airport where you can purchase frozen
barbecue in compact carry-on Styrofoam containers for
what seems to be an obscene price.

I ordered pork ribs at the original Corky's location.
The pork barbecue was advertised as "slow-cooked, can
be pulled from the bone in tender shreds, doused in

tangy sauce, and piled on steam buns – with a mound of ice-cold coleslaw as garnish." Really tasty and tender, but nothing spectacular, $11.95 + tax. It was in an old, single-story building with little parking space. There were lots of framed 8 X 10 pictures of celebrities on the walls: Dan Quayle, Bill Clinton, former Miss Americas, Pau Gasol, Andy Roddick, Shane Battier, Vlade Divac with a white long-sleeved shirt and a psychedelic tie. There were many other celebrities with their pictures on the wall. The management did not ask to take my picture.

On the way back to the airport the driver of the car rental courtesy van was telling me about a very huge, he said HUGE, convention coming up. Every year in November, conventioneers, called "saints" of the Church of God in Christ (COGIC), congregate in Memphis to wash the downtown city streets and sidewalks in a sea of stylish hats, bejeweled dresses and fine suits. An estimated 60,000 saints were expected for the event. I had to get out of town. I quickly took my flight to Dallas and on to Sacramento.

THE SNIPER

I didn't forget the sniper. A wedding guest who lived in Memphis gave me directions from the cathedral to Germantown. Go east on Central, north on East Parkway, east on Poplar and so on. He specifically said I should avoid Sam Cooper Boulevard because there was a sniper on the loose. I disregarded his advice and took Sam Cooper anyway.

I got lucky.

I survived the sniper in Memphis and lived to tell this story.

DEEP IN THE
HEART OF TEJAS

L ast May, I visited the city of San Antonio (originally San Antonio de Béxar), Texas, (or Tejas, as the Mexicans called that northern province in the old days). The "de Béxar" has been dropped from the city name, but Béxar was the name adopted by the county.

There are no non-stop flights to San Antonio from Sacramento. I selected flights with a stopover in Phoenix, Arizona. At the stopover in Phoenix, I was tempted to buy an NBA Phoenix Suns T-shirt at the obscene price of $19.99. That was before the Sun set on Phoenix in the NBA Western Finals. I yielded to the temptation, so now I own the used, overpriced T-shirt of a loser team.

As with most airport stores, prices in the shops in Phoenix Sky Harbor Airport are outrageously expensive. Free market and price competition mean nothing to them. The Burger King miniature breakfast item + tater tots + tiny coffee cup was $6.00. And please don't forget the tax. I knew I should have brought a more tasty and nutritious homemade sandwich with me.

Everyone's Home

It is said that all Texans have two homes, their hometown and San Antonio. While San Antonio is not the geographic center of Texas, it is a great cultural and historical city. It is the only large city that was established long before Texas gained independence from Mexico in 1836. Texas was annexed as the 28th US state in 1845, just a few years before California. Of San Antonio's over 1.1 million people, about 60 percent are Hispanic. Not unexpectedly, many street names are Spanish like Navarro, La Villita, Santa Rosa, Flores, and San Pedro.

Many Polish and Germans settled in the area in the mid 1800s. It is said that the most widely spoken languages in San Antonio, in order of decreasing popularity, are Spanish, English, German, and Polish. Could this area have the largest population of Polish surnames outside of Chicago and Poland itself? On freeway signs along Hwy 35 to Austin, many German names can be seen indicating towns, roads, exits and the like. Schertz. Rittiman. Eisenhauer. Teopperwein. Niederwald. Conrads. Schlitterbahn. Wurzbach. Maltsberger. Bracken. I did not see a street or town named Schwarzenegger.

The Alamo

Well it was there I found, beside the Alamo,
Enchantments strange as the blue up above.
-The Rose of San Antone

The Alamo is best remembered for the supreme heroic resistance by the Alamo defense force against the Mexicans in 1836. For thirteen days, Davy Crockett, James Bowie, Col. William B. Travis and their courageous cohorts battled the forces of Mexican General Antonio Lopez de Santa Anna.

A LITTLE BACKGROUND
Several battles were fought in the San Antonio area during the Mexican Revolution 1810 – 1821. Forces loyal to the King of Spain fought continually against the forces intent on establishing an independent Mexico.

Sometime in the 1820s a Mr. Moses Austin arrived in San Antonio and requested permission from the Spanish governor to settle some three hundred families in Texas. The request was initially denied in large part due to Spanish dislike of Anglos. The request was eventually granted and that started the flood of Anglo settlement into Texas and the west. The new settlers were required to become Catholics and acquire Mexican citizenship. All the new settlers accepted these conditions, even if their allegiance was not to Mexico.

In due time, the idea of independence began to sprout all over Texas. When the Mexican military, under General de Cos, occupied San Antonio and attempted to suppress the idea of an independent Texas, the locals overran them. General de Cos surrendered. This event incensed General Santa Anna who was also the Mexican President at that time. He therefore assembled an attack force and led them himself to the Alamo at San Antonio.

Though all the Alamo defenders died in their heroic fight against Santa Anna's much larger attack force, they nevertheless seriously weakened Santa Anna's forces. The

Alamo defenders did not know that while they held the Alamo, Texans had already declared independence from Mexico. Another band of Texans later defeated Santa Anna's forces in the Battle of San Jacinto and secured their independence from Mexico. That's a short version of a long story.

When Santa Anna's forces annihilated all the Alamo defenders, their bodies were left lying where they fell; there were no friendly forces around to bury them. So the history goes that Santa Anna ordered all the Texas dead burned. There are many stories about mysterious happenings and strange noises in the Alamo area. Some attribute these to the dead who were killed in sudden and violent fighting and denied a Christian burial.

THE ALAMO

This historic complex is not in a secluded, out of the way area of San Antonio. The mission is right in the heart of the present day San Antonio downtown. And guess what? It's on a road named Alamo Street! There is a tiny plaza right in front of the Alamo and crossing the street, you will find shops and hotels and restaurants. The Spanish founded it around 1724, as Mission San Antonio de Valero. Later, military occupants eventually assigned the moniker "Alamo." Spanish officials eventually secularized the mission and distributed the land among their converts, basically similar to the secularization process implemented for California missions.

The (old) Alamo dome is a very huge stadium where the San Antonio Spurs, among other teams, played a couple of years back. It's no more than two miles from the convention center. Though there did not seem to be anything wrong with it, they built the newer and better SBC Center in 2006 (renamed AT&T Center). It is located on a plot of land about five miles east of downtown San Antonio in an area surrounded by empty land with overgrown weeds, older warehouses, older homes and an occasional tavern where Spurs fans gather to cheer for their team.

San Antonio has a tower like the Seattle Space Needle and the Stratosphere in Las Vegas. They call it the Tower of the Americas. It is located inside the Hemis Fair Park, just behind the Henry B. Gonzales Convention Center. As expected, both the park and convention center are run by government entities with matching levels of service. I think you know what I mean. During my visit, there was a conference of purchasing managers at the convention center and one weekend, there was no coffee concession open. The convention center management told the organizing committee that the coffee concessions do not operate on weekends, even if there is a convention!

The Tower of the Americas was a great disappointment. It was due for renovation and as of this writing is probably closed to the public. It had a very shabby ground floor entrance and a squeaky, shaky elevator that brought me to the top. Up top, the windows were dirty – how was I supposed to view the San Antonio cityscape through blurry windows? The gift shop atop was abandoned with locked shelves, leftover souvenirs, and postcards. The snack bar was closed; the vending machine was not working. If you visit, check first to see if they're open before you spend time (about fifteen minutes) walking through the park to the tower.

THE RIVERWALK

When I took the mandatory boat ride along the famed San Antonio Riverwalk, the driver/guide/comedian bragged that it was the most visited spot in all of Texas. It supposedly generates over $9 billion annually. To me, that was an unmistakable indication that the dozens of restaurants and hotels and souvenir shops along its path are tourist traps. I checked out the shops along the Riverwalk. I was not mistaken.

The usual restaurants line the Riverwalk. Italian. Mexican. American. Souvenir shops with overpriced items. Some river boats had dining tables with white tablecloths and elegant place settings. These were the dinner cruise boats. Food is brought on to the boats from a restaurant, and diners enjoy the ride while having their dinner. Some boats cook food on board. It is totally possible that some drops of water from the river may sprinkle on your food without your knowing it. Be aware that foods in towns you visit may cause some grumbling stomach.

In Bangkok Thailand, they have a similar tourist attraction on a river called the floating market. The main activity is trading fruits and other food items among boats, but tourists can join a boat trip and eat local fruits and other foods too. Some foods can cause food poisoning, depending on the tourist's resistance to unfamiliar bacteria.

Old Sacramento has a riverfront area, too, but with fewer restaurants. The Rio City Café is on the water on First Street, and there is the restaurant on the Delta King paddleboat. There are other spots on Garden Highway along the river. Now that I'm thinking about it, Milwaukee, Wisconsin, has a Riverwalk, and Kansas City, Missouri, has a market at the north end of downtown which they call River Market. I guess since towns tend to sprout along riverbanks, at one time or another, they all have a "river something."

On the east wide of San Antonio is a cluster of Mexican products and souvenir shops around El Mercado. A mandatory tourist stop here is the 70-year old restaurant, Mi Tierra, that is open 24/7. (The family has two other restaurants close by.) It is said to serve the tastiest genuine Mexican food in town. I was told the wait is usually forty minutes. I registered at the counter and they gave me a number on a card. Since there could be about a hundred people waiting at any one time, they do not call out your number. You merely have to look up at the lighted panels (like pharmacy prescription lights) atop the corners of the restaurant and the adjoining bar. I was alone so maybe that's why they got me a table quicker, inside twenty minutes.

The food was tasty though not spectacular. The restaurant has a fun fiesta atmosphere – colorful pennants and balloons on the ceiling, Mexican music non-stop, loud conversation non-stop. Vendors in native Mexican attire wander among tables selling all types of children's toys, lighted twirly things, masks, horns. Photographers with tall hats ask if you want your picture taken. Flower vendors sell both fresh and silk flowers. Shelves at the cashier's counter sport different styles of Mi Tierra t-shirts, at tourist prices of course. Signs warn the patio diners not to feed the ubiquitous pigeons just outside the patio railing. Outside the restaurant, other vendors sell similar toys, drinks and Mexican fast food. By the way, if you have a brown complexion, you are expected to *habla Español*.

AUSTIN, TEXAS

Austin, the Texas state capital, about seventy-two miles northeast of San Antonio, is the home of the University of Texas (UT). Austin has a well-known party town atmosphere, I imagine in large part because of the student population. On Friday nights, several blocks of downtown around 6th Street have anything and everything by way of music, food, beverage – adult and otherwise. As a visual incentive for the partying students to behave, police cars patrol the area constantly.

Do you remember LBJ ? Well, that's Lyndon Baines Johnson, a one-time Texas Senator who was John Fitzgerald Kennedy's Vice-President in the early 60s. When JFK was assassinated in Dallas in November, 1963, LBJ took over as president, taking the oath of office on board Air Force One which was flying back to Washington DC.

The Lyndon Baines Johnson Presidential Library is on east side of UT. It houses the usual presidential library material: biographical exhibits, a sampling of gifts from foreign dignitaries and Americans. When I visited, there was an exhibit of all things 60s – flower power artwork, tie-dyed shirts, funky music, Beatles, VW Kombi, rebel authors of the era and more.

There is another presidential library in the area, about 150 miles from San Antonio. It's the (father of Dubya) George Bush Presidential Library and Museum in College Station, TX, also the home of Texas A & M University. I was told the "A" and "M" stand for Agriculture and Mechanical.

Perhaps a little-known fact about presidential libraries is that they all get (are entitled to) some federal money, in addition to private donations they raise themselves. The Richard Nixon Birthplace and Library in Yorba Linda, CA, claims not to receive any federal money. However, it is known that part of the land where the library stands was donated by the city of Yorba Linda, CA, to the Nixon library. Personally, I object to giving any public thing (federal or local) to private institutions. Whatever.

The current President Bush's ranch in Crawford TX is near Waco, some 95 miles northeast of Austin. That was too far for me to drive for an unannounced visit.

LARGEST CAPITOL IN THE US

True to form, the Texas state capitol building in Austin is the largest capitol in the nation. It is even larger than the US Capitol. It covers over eight acres of floor space. Its height is 302.64 feet – that's 14.64 feet taller than the U.S. Capitol. A portrait painting of a former one-term governor named George W. Bush hangs in the lobby along with all the other past governors.

WHY THE TERM "SIX FLAGS OVER TEXAS ?"

The history is that there have been six national flags over Texas since the first European exploration around 1517. First was Texas under Spain. Second was a Texas flag under France. Third was a Texas flag under Mexico. Fourth was a Texas flag as a Republic after it gained independence from Mexico but before it joined the Union. Fifth was a Texas flag as part of the Confederacy. Sixth is Texas as part of the current United States of America. So there.

Here's a little advice for travelers. When planning a trip, it's always a good idea to read up and research the places you will visit *before* you go. I promise you there will be little time to read up on the place when you arrive. If I had remembered the fun Friday nights at Austin, I could have booked a room there for the day of my arrival. I hear there are lots of sports bars and music places there. The students in Austin really know how to party. I consider that a missed opportunity.

And here's something I learned *after* I came back home: there is a Filipino restaurant near downtown San Antonio called "Cebu Philippines." Another tip: if you want to avoid the high tourist prices of local souvenirs like t-shirts, you can try the Walgreens or Rite-Aids or Wal-Marts in the area. They generally have nice souvenirs at about half the price. Finally, don't forget it's not against the law to bring a sandwich and a drink on the plane if you want to avoid the obscene prices of unhealthy foods at most airports.

Use the Right Word; Put the Accent on the Correct Sylláble

All languages have some form of spoken characteristics that distinguish certain words from others that have the same or similar sounds. I'm sure people who study this particular field have names for these spoken characteristics – inflection, accent, tones, whatever.

Aside from tone, some words in Philippine languages, like Mandarin Chinese, mean different things in different parts of the country.

In Mandarin Chinese, the word *mai* can mean either buy or sell depending on the tone. A heavy downward tone *mài* means sell, while an upward tone *mái* means buy. This can really be a delicate matter when giving instructions on the stock exchange.

In the Bicol region, the word *kawat* means to play. But be careful when you use that word with the exact same inflection and accent in Cebu because there it means to steal. And there is the eternal story in which one brags about his town where *tanán "pusod" may pulis* (at every "corner" there is a policeman). The required response about your own town is: *tanán pulis, may "pusod"* (every policeman has a "bellybutton"). Same word: pusod. Totally different meaning: (street)corner vs. bellybutton.

In Beijing *hai-dz* means child while in another part of China, it means shoes. You should therefore be extremely careful in the subway or on a crowded bus when shouting out, "I've lost my *hai-dz*!"

A ubiquitous banner in industrial plants all over China proclaims: *An Chuan Ti Yi,* which translates into "Safety First!" Well, if you mispronounce – as many foreigners do - the *an chuan* as *an chun,* you are liable to proclaim the totally irrelevant slogan, "Quails First!" The word *an chun* means quail – you know, as in quail eggs, the delicacy. So there, please mind your pronunciation!

So now, try to speak out and enunciate clearly these words below. Move your lips. Put the accent on what you consider to be the right syllable. Then make various changes on the placement of the accent or intonation. I have included words that have similar beginning or ending sounds. The references to Tagalog or Cebuano or Bicol are approximate – certainly imperfect due to the writer's inadequate knowledge. The accents and words can well be available in many other regional dialects and languages.

Remember all vowels are pronounced short. "A" sound is like "car." "I" sound like "pin." "O" sound as in "pro."

"U" sounds like a double "o." Each group has words that are related by sound, meaning, accent or some other attribute. The space on the right is for you to fill in other words that come to mind. Have fun !

Abay   escort, best man
Abáy   to sleep beside someone, something

Ahit   shave (a beard), colloquial: a close call
Ha-it   sharp, Cebuano

Alúk   offer
Alak   liquor

Anino   shadow
Kanino   whose ?

Halakhak loud laughter
Halík   kiss

Alám   to know
Ulam   a food dish, viand
Alamát   legend

Asa   hope, expectation
Asa   where, Cebuano
Asal   behavior, manner
Asál   roast, as in a pig

Asín   salt
Asim   degree of sourness

Asawa   spouse, either wife or husband (Tagalog)
Asawa   wife, Visayan

Ed Palenque

Bana   husband, Visayan

Mag-asawa a married couple, Tagalog
Mag-ti-ayon a married couple, Cebuano

Ayaw   don't want
Away   fight
Yawà   demon

Babà   chin
Babâ   to go down (downstairs)
Babalâ   a warning notice

Baga   ember
Bagà   lung
Bagá   extra word used to emphasize
Bagâ   thick, Cebuano

Bagay   a thing, something
Bagay   befitting, be suitable
Bagáy   a (boxing) brawl, Cebuano

Bagsik   harshness, aggressiveness
Bagsák   to drop or fall

Baka   a cow, struggle (as in "makibaka")
Baká   perhaps, maybe

Balak   a plan (to do something)
Bulak   cotton

Balát   skin, leather
Balat   birthmark (?)
Balag   a trellis or arbor
Balík   to return

Balot   wrapper
Balót   duck egg (semi-hatched)

Bangâ   a water container, Tagalog
Bangâ   mentally deficient, Cebuano

Basa   to read
Basâ   wet

Bata   bath robe
Batà   young, a young one, a child
Butá   bling (Visayan)

Batí   to beat, stir
Batì   greeting
Batî   to be on good terms with someone

Bilís   speed
Bilás   brother-in-law

Bugtong   a riddle
Dugtong   a connection

Buháy   alive
Buhay   life
Báhay   house

Bukas   tomorrow
Bukás   open

Buko   bud of a flower, young coconut
Bukó   to fail, to be found out (doing wrong)

Ed Palenque

Da-án   road
Da-án   hundred
Da-an   old, Cebuano

Dagâ   rat
Dagâ   plot of land (Bicol)

Dagan   run, Cebuano
Dagán   restrain down with one's weight, Tagalog

Dako   a location, a place
Dakô   large, huge, Cebuano

Dalá   anything carried, a load
Dalâ   disappointment, a bad experience

Dalág   a type of fish
Dalaga   maiden, unmarried lady

Dalás   frequently
Dulás   slide on slick surface
Malas   bad luck (from Spanish)

Damó   Grass
Damò   Plenty, Visayan

Gabí   night time, Tagalog
Gabí-i   night time, Cebuano
Gabi   type of root crop

Gamót   medicine, Tagalog
Gamót   root of a plant, Cebuano

Hawak   to hold, a hold on something
Hawak   waist, Cebuano

Ibá   different
Ibá   to come along, Bicol

Ikáw   a form of "you" (second person singular)
Hikaw   earring

Ilog   a river
Ilag   to dodge, duck

Ilaw   light
Silaw   to be blinded by light

Kamó   a form of "you", Cebuano (second person plural)
Kamót   hand, Cebuano
Kamot   to scratch (an itch), Tagalog

Kayó   a form of "you" (second person plural)
Kayo   fire, Cebuano

Kilay   eyebrow
Likáy   to duck, evade, Cebuano
Kulay   color

Labay   to throw away, Visayan
Labáy   to pass by (along the way), Visayan

Ligaw   to court (a lady)
Ligáw   lose one's way
Lugaw   rice porridge

Matá   eyes
Tamà   correct, a hit

Pa-á   Feet, Tagalog
Pa-a   Leg, Cebuano

Ed Palenque

Panit   skin, Cebuano
Anit   scalp, Tagalog
Pangit   ugly

Pasa   to pass on
Pasá   to pass, say, an examination
Pasâ   a skin blemish
Pusà   cat, Tagalog

Paták   drop, as in raindrop
Patakà   slipshod, careless manner, Cebuano
Pitaka   purse

Payo   advice
Payó   face, Bicol
Payong   umbrella

Pasáyan   type of shrimp, Cebuano
Pasyálan   leisurely walk (?)
Syalan   ? what's going on ? Dumaguete (?)

Pila   a line, queue
Pilá   how much, how many, Cebuano

Pilit   force
Pilít   to stick, adhere, Cebuano

Pintô   door
Punta   to go somewhere
Puntó   accent, as a distinctive tone of a dialect
Pinta   to paint

Salo   to get together
Saló   to catch something (like a ball)

Sandál   to lean on
Sandalan   back rest
Dasál   pray

Sangáy   (tree) branch
Sungay   horn (like the devil's)
Sigáy   seashell

Simbá   attend church
Simbahan   church
Samba   to worship

Sudlay   hair comb, Visayan
Suklay   hair comb, Tagalog

Suki   one with whom you have a regular business relationship
Kusî   to pinch, Cebuano

Sukà   vinegar
Suka   what comes out of your mouth when you get sick
(yuks!)
Kusa   of one's own volition

Sungkâ   a game similar to mancala
Sampal   slap
Sampalan   a slapping orgy (!)

Sampay   to hang (to dry, as in clothes) Tagalog
Sampayan   clothes (drying) line
Sumpay   to connect, Cebuano

Sukò   surrender
Sukô   be angry, Cebuano
Sukol   to take on (as in fight)

Ed Palenque

Sisi   regret, Tagalog
Susì   key, likely from the Chinese "yao sz"
Llave   key, Cebuano, from Spanish

Tabang help, Cebuano
Tabáng bland taste, Tagalog

Tangan hold, Tagalog
Tangá   naïve, Tagalog, also tange, ta-nge-ngot

Tapon   to throw away
Tapón   a cap, cover for a container like a bottle cap
Tabón   a cover, Cebuano

Tainga (or tenga) ear (as in what Vincent lost)
Tingá   food particles embedded between teeth

Tayô   to stand
Tayo   Us, we

Toyò   soy sauce – most probably from Chinese "chiang
you"
Tuyô   dry (not wet)

Ugá   dry, Cebuano
Ugâ   to shake, Tagalog

Ulap   a cloud
Ulán   rain
Ulam   a food dish, viand

You May Be Getting
Old When.......

We're not as young as we once were. We never are. Every minute that passes ages us, some ways visibly, other ways not so visible. To assess your geriatric status, use the self-assessment questionnaire below. You know you're getting old when.....

- ❑ You're now sleeping with a *lolo* (grandpa). Or a *lola* (grandma).
- ❑ You're on the hit list of AARP.
- ❑ Or you're now enjoying their too-numerous-to-mention benefits.
- ❑ The only whistles you get are from the teakettle.
- ❑ You now know the difference between HDL and LDL.
- ❑ You automatically receive an Estimated Benefits Statement from SSA.
- ❑ You don't need an alarm clock to wake up with the chickens.
- ❑ Your children are getting to like you again.
- ❑ You now know the meaning of *diastolic* and *systolic*.

- They're doing some things on TV that you didn't even do on your wedding night.
- You now allow you husband to hold the TV remote.
- You need a special fire permit to light all your birthday candles.
- And you need oxygen after blowing them out.
- You have more medicine in your fridge than...beer
- You drop off your dry cleaning at the post office.
- You get winded playing checkers.
- Your gray hair has more body.
- You sit in a rocking chair and can't get it going.
- People make fun of your musical taste – lots of Lawrence Welk... And you get offended.
- You have lots of stories about World War II.
- Your phone list contains only names ending with M.D.
- Everything hurts. And what doesn't hurt, doesn't work.
- Your pacemaker opens the garage door whenever a cute girl goes by.
- You don't know any "rap" or "hip-hop" artists.
- You put on your reading glasses to listen to books on tape.
- You have too much room in the house, and not enough in the medicine cabinet.
- You buy cereal *not* for the toy, but for the fiber content.
- You want to wear high-heels but your back aches more and stays sore for days.
- A bad hair day refers to the hair growing out of your nose and ears.
- Your children begin to impose a curfew on *you*.
- You don't know how to send text messages.
- You accept being bald and see the bright side – there's no need to wash your hair anymore.
- You're the only one sober enough to drive home after a wild party.
- You think menopause entitles you to park in the

handicap zone.

❑ You know what a computer looks like but you don't know how to turn it on.

❑ More than half your income is from winning sports pools.

❑ Your wife offers to help you change a flat.

❑ You're happy there are many mysteries in large print.

❑ Everyone keeps telling you you're driving too slowly.

❑ You keep telling everyone they're driving too fast.

❑ Now *you're* the backseat driver.

❑ You don't know what email is.

❑ Your ties are back in style.

❑ A chewy bagel cracks a molar.

❑ You don't know the lyrics of any of Britney Spears songs.

❑ Heck, you don't even know who Britney Spears is.

❑ You keep telling people, "When I was your age...."

❑ Your car radio is pre-set to the oldies stations.

❑ Your kids are through college. And they're making more than you.

❑ You need your glasses to find your glasses.

❑ You don't know what "phat" or "bling" means.

❑ You notice everyone is dressed different than you.

❑ Your wife no longer grills you about new secretaries at work.

❑ You often say at work, "We already tried that and it didn't work."

❑ The pinpricks on your jacket were made by Nixon campaign buttons.

❑ CD doesn't mean a music Compact Disc to you - you only know it as Certificate of Deposit.

❑ Blowing up party balloons gets you winded.

❑ You can't see the bathroom scale without your glasses.

❑ And even with your glasses, your tummy blocks the view of said bathroom scale.

❑ You're the only one who remembers the office

Christmas party of 1972.

❑ You feel like the "morning after" when you haven't been anywhere the night before.

And one unmistakable sign that you may be getting old...

❑ Even your doctor is dead.

DOBLE – DOBLE

There is a class of words in the Filipino language which are formed by repeating the word itself. For example, the word *birò* (jest, joke) would become: *biro-birò*. The new word now has a slightly changed meaning: joking around.

This word form appears to be common in various Filipino dialects. Just listen and observe when Filipinos are talking. Sooner or later, there is bound to be a word that is *doble-doble*. Try this out and I promise you when a *doble-doble* word is spoken, you will break into a wide smile !

I don't know if there is a technical name for this word form. I really have no idea how this repetitious word form developed. It looks like some of the Tagalog word roots are nouns or verbs and the repetition converts them into other word forms. It seems the repetition emphasizes the original single word or, in some case, diminishes the essence! In some cases though, it seems that's just the original form of the word like *ala-ala* which translates to 'memory.'

Mandarin Chinese seems to have something similar. The word *gao* means tall; and the conversion into *gao-gao* sort of denotes somewhat tall. And the word *kan* means to see, while *kan-kan* is used to mean have a look-see. A similar conversion occurs in Bicol when you repeat the last syllable to indicate comparative or superlative degrees. *Magayon* (beautiful) is *magayon-non* (very beautiful). Extremely beautiful is *magayon-no-no-......-no-non..*

I've decided to call this repetition word form "doble-doble." Pronounce this as "dob" and "le." Do not pronounce this like the word "double." The only example of this word form in English that comes to mind is the word "no-no." The sounds have to be exactly the same. So "dilly-dally" does not qualify as a *doble-doble*; neither does "sing-song."

Sidebar on pronunciation: Remember, the vowels in Tagalog words are always pronounced <u>short</u>. "A" as in "Car." "O" as in musical "Do." "I" as in "Indian." Also, <u>all</u> consonants and <u>all</u> individual vowels are vocalized – it's as phonetic as you can get. Pronouncing the words correctly makes reading this repetition word form more fun and authentic.

Many of you surely have more precise definitions for these Tagalog words. Send them to me please so we can refine and expand this list. In the meantime, have fun !

Agad-agad   Instantly, quickly
Ala-ala   Memory
Akay-akay   Tugging along

Araw-araw   Daily
Bagay-bagay Stuff, thingy
Bakó-bakó Uneven surface, as in describing a road
Bali-balí All broken to pieces – as in broken sticks
Balic-Balic   To and fro
Barong-barong Austere dwelling made of indigenous material
Barrio-barrio Tending to be insular, parochial, provincial, narrow-minded
Baság-baság All broken to pieces – as a broken clay pot
Bay-bay   Beach
Bil-bil   Body fat, cellulite
Bilóg-bilóg   Any round thingy
Bini-bini   Unmarried lady
Biro-biro   Just kidding, horsing around
Bit-bit   Carrying a light item
Bog-bog   To maul, mug
Bong-bong   Wall (Cebuano)
Buhat-buhat Carrying a medium heavy item
Buk-buk   Termite, rot
Bulóng-bulóng Whispering
Buwan-buwan Monthly
Dag-dag   Additional
Dahan-dahan Slowly
Dala-dala   Carrying, things being carried
Dib-dib   Chest
Dikit-dikit   Many, very closely stuck together
Dili-dili   Hesitate, hesitation
Ding-ding   Wall
Doble-doble   Duplicated
Dugtóng-dugtóng Many, connected to each other
Gabi-gabi   Nightly
Gamit-gamit Use, utensils, tools
Gas-gas   Scratch on an object
Gaw-gaw   a type of starch

Gong-gong   Unintelligent, stupid, feeble-minded
Hakot-hakot Hauling stuff
Halo-halo A mix – of whatever; also: shaved ice + various sweet fruits shake
Hasa-hasa   A kind of fish
Hati-hati   To divide, not necessarily equally
Hawak-hawak Holding on to something
Hay-Hay   Clothes on a clothesline (Cebuano)
Hila-hila   Pulling
Hinay-hinay Slowly (Visayan)
Hong-hong   Whisper (Cebuano)
Hula-hulà   Guessing
Ibá-ibá   All Different
Ikot-ikot   Going round in circles
Ipil-ipil   A kind of tree
Ipit-ipit   Squeezed in tweezer-like device
Isa-isa One at a time, also for many other numbers
Kal-kal   Dig
Karga-karga Carrying around on one's arms or shoulders
Kay-kay   Rake – noun or verb
Kili-kili   Armpit
Kit-kit   Gnaw at
Kompol-kompol Lumped together
Kuláng-kuláng Incomplete, missing something; also a mental retardation
Lag-lag To drop
Lagay-lagay Situation; also connotes grease money
Lagi-lagi   Always and ever, perennial
Lay-lay   Loose, hanging
Lib-lib Out in the boondocks, away from it all
Ligoy-ligoy   Sauntering aimlessly
Liko-liko Random crooked direction, going every which way
Linggo-Linggo Weekly
Loko-loko   Crazy, confused

Lubak-Lubak   Uneven surface, as in describing a road
(see Bakó-bakó)
Luray-luray   Smashed, dilapidated (?)
Me-me   Lull to sleep
Ngit-ngit   Dark, as in night (Visayan)
Pal-pal   Block a shot – as in basketball
Pak-Pak   Wings with which to fly, to clap (Cebuano)
Pas-pas   Device to drive away flies; also Palm Sunday
Pat-pat   A thin stick
Patay-patay   Unconcerned, I-don't-care behavior, aka
government work
Patong-patong   On top of one another
Pay-pay   Fan
Pud-pud   Worn out
Punit-punit   All torn
Sabáy-sabáy   Altogether, in unison
Sabi-sabi   Gossip, rumor, scuttlebutt
Sabit-sabit   Stuff hanging all around
Salo-salo   Get-together
Sama-sama   Altogether
Sapín-sapín   Layered gummy rainbow-colored sweet delicacy
Sap-sap   A kind of fish
Sari-sari   A wide variety; as in Sari Sari Store
Si-si   To blame, to regret
Sik-sik   To squeeze into
Sing-sing   Ring
Sino-sino   Whoever
Siping-siping   Lying beside each other
Sip-sip   Denotes "to suck"; connotes "to kiss up"
Sulok-sulok   Nooks and crannies
Sunód-sunód   One after another
Sup-sup   Synonym of sip-sip (to kiss up)
Suson-suson   Carrying atop one's head
Tabi-tabi   Many beside each other
Tangan-tangan   Holding an item

Taón-taón   Yearly
Tayo-tayo   Us all
Tingín-tingín Look see
Ting-ting   Very thin stick – as in the stripped spine of coconut leaves
Tok-tok   Knock (on a door), on a very high spot
Tulak-tulak   Being pushed
Turo-turo Diner – where one points (turo) to order food
Ulit-ulit   Repetition
Yaw-yaw Meaningless loud talk (Visayan), nagging

THE IGNORANT IMMIGRANT

The typical depiction of a new immigrant shows a person with crumpled clothing, messy hair, bleary eyes, tugging beat-up luggage, holding tight to precious documents that authorize admission into the new country. Wide-eyed, surveying unfamiliar surroundings, the new immigrant has a half-smile and is ready to take on the adopted country with high hopes and great expectations of future happiness and bliss.

Alas, the new immigrant soon finds out that the new country is not all it's cracked up to be. The new country is not the land of the free that he's envisioned. The new immigrant quickly finds out that everywhere, everyone is constantly asking the government to side with them to trample on *other* people's rights and property and liberty and pursuit of happiness.

I sympathize with the ignorant immigrant. Being an ignorant immigrant myself, there are many things I do not understand. I hope the reader can explain what's going on.

RIGHT TO VOTE

Many people make a big deal about exercising the right to vote. Any idiot knows, me included, that voting won't make a bit of difference in what legislators will do once they are elected. Votes never have, votes never will. What happens is constant horse-trading in the legislature, be it at the town, city or state level, or in Washington. Countless lobby groups (Sacramento is a big-time influence peddler town) spend obscene amounts of money and time to influence politicians to legislate in their favor. Politicians know that the common people (that's you and me) are usually not organized so it does not hurt to ignore them. That is, except in speeches.

Politicians curry favor with the lobby groups because they have the money to cause trouble, and trouble is the last thing a politician wants. Lobby groups can create trouble for politicians in many ways, from issuing unflattering press releases, to withholding campaign contributions, to threatening to withhold their members' votes. No politician wants trouble. Also, it costs nothing for the politician to accede to lobby groups' requests, and even if it did, those costs would be borne by the (ha ha) taxpayers (that's you and me). The ignorant immigrant is naïve to believe that the common people have a chance. Am I right or am I right ?

SHORTAGES

The ignorant immigrant wonders why there is often a shortage of some critical item in the economy – say, flu vaccine. In centrally planned economies, of which there are relatively few remaining, a central planning group decides what items will be produced by what parts of the country. Like in the old USSR, a central planning group decided how many refrigerators would be produced, which provinces would produce which components, etc. The premise of such a system is that the central planners know the supply and demand situation better than anybody else. The ignorant immigrant wonders how this can be.

A vibrant economy is necessarily constantly changing. If consumers go about their life, always trying to get a good deal and rejecting unwanted products and services, the marketplace (sellers) will automatically adjust. Sellers will offer popular products and will abandon unpopular ones. They are driven by self-interest: to make money. In short time, consumers will see more of the products they want and sellers will make more money. In a sense, consumers vote for products by paying for them, and sellers who want to make money respond quickly to the vote tally.

Isn't it amazing that when buyers and sellers pursue their own self-interest, the economy gets going and the most wanted products and services are somehow inevitably made available?

I know there is no way a huge bureaucracy can possibly see everything going on in the market in a timely manner – even if there is a huge government data-gathering superstructure. Some call central economic planning socialist, though this was a feature of many communist countries in days past. I believe the explanation of Adam Smith. He stated that when people go about their own business trying to get the best deal they can, market forces will automatically adjust supply of items to the demand – "as if guided by an invisible hand."

The USA, being the land of plenty surely can do anything and everything all the time. Except - flu vaccine during peak demand season. The ignorant immigrant wonders why. Could it be that some government bureaucrat or committee who lacks judgement (redundancy intentional) is involved somewhere in the process?

Who has ever heard of a shortage of KFC chicken, or McDonald's burgers, or Pepsi, or Nike shoes, or Taco Bell burritos, or cell phones, or video games, or tennis balls, (Sacramento NBA) Kings jerseys ? My question stands: Why do we run out of flu vaccine ?

I imagine there is some elaborate government bureaucracy created to protect the public from "bad" medicine, and that it does indeed take a lot of time to approve new vaccines. We often read news about a recently approved medicine that will save X thousand lives per year. And the approval took, say, eight years or something like that. Has anyone ever wondered about the lives that were lost due to the approval bureaucracy? (X thousand lives per year, times years delayed.) Someone please educate this ignorant immigrant.

PUBLIC SCHOOLS

It seems to me that teacher's associations and educational administrators have been given a monopoly in determining how government funds for schools are to be spent. In case you didn't know, the amount of annual funds appropriated for education is a gazillion times the net worth of our dear friend Bill Gates! Where does it say and how did it come to pass that this small, artificially created group of people have the exclusive right to say how that staggering amount of money will be spent? I'm sure someone will say it's the law. May I then inquire about who proposed said laws in the first place?

A terribly weak effort is made to reassure parents' groups. They are invited to be active in school affairs, to make suggestions and blah, blah, blah. But everyone knows that's just talk – all substantial decisions on spending are ultimately made by the know-it-all bureaucrats, politicians and the special interest groups that pressure them.

I had occasion to chat with a woman who I didn't know was a public school teacher. I registered my inclination toward school vouchers where parents are given the power to decide where to send their children to school. I was surprised (because I am naïve) when the schoolteacher said she was not in favor of vouchers. She said it's because she's a *public* school teacher. Pretending not to understand her objection, I tried to explain to her how she could actually have an advantage with school vouchers.

I said as a public school teacher, she has more credentials and training than other less qualified teachers. So, in an open (voucher) market for schools, she would be given preference in hiring, assignment, seniority, etc. If I were a public school teacher, I said, I would embrace vouchers. She didn't budge; she was still against vouchers.

Now, I'm wondering if she actually realizes, deep in her heart, that her credentials are artificial. She is not brainless. In all likelihood she actually knows that her credentials will probably have no currency (no real value) in an open market situation. You know, she could be right. Dang. I know she's right.

Teacher certifications and related credential requirements are viewed by many as meaningless, the result of laws enacted through heavy lobbying by teachers' groups over the years. They have no intrinsic value, none whatsoever. Credentials acquire value only when a law makes it a prerequisite (among many other bureaucratic requirements) for teaching. The credentials are no more than artificially created barriers, created to enlarge the scope and power of teachers' groups.

If you really want to determine the effectiveness of teachers' credentials, just look at the quality of most students graduating from public schools. Don't just listen to this misinformed and ignorant immigrant, look at the products of public schools. Then, decide for yourself.

PUBLIC LIBRARIES

Recent news articles mention community outcry and concern about diminishing funding for public libraries. As for this ignorant immigrant, I really don't care. I do hope though that I get some money back from the taxes I pay. Now, before you castigate me for being against libraries and their accompanying benefits for the public good, please note there is a difference between libraries and public libraries.

Though they are not as well known, there are many nonpublic libraries around - libraries financed by private entities, corporate libraries, libraries funded and run by private foundations, as well as by private schools, colleges and universities. There are countless libraries and bookstores with free browsing if you buy a cup of latté, etc. So why have we been conditioned to think of libraries as the exclusive domain of the government?

The ignorant immigrant quickly noticed in this country the extremely tolerant and ambivalent attitude of most people towards religion – any kind of religion. It's almost as if people are saying, "You do your religion, I do mine. I don't bother you, you don't bother me. Everyone's cool." This is a good thing. Yet we do hear complaints about public libraries carrying this or that kind of reading material. I can only imagine the amount of bureaucracy involved in deciding what kind of books should be allowed in public libraries. Here again, a few all-knowing bureaucrats are deciding what is good for the general public.

WORKING FOR THE GOVERNMENT

Why do government workers get more money than people in private business? A recent article on baby boomers close to retirement mentioned a certain Ms. so-and-so. "Like most people who work for a government agency or public-education entity," the article said, "her retirement benefits will be substantial, even without Social Security." Is it only me who finds this statement extremely offensive? It is offensive because it is true and the government continues to ride on the backs of ordinary common workers and small businesses. I have no objection to private businesses providing obscenely high salaries and benefits to their employees. Private businesses compete in the open market – against other like businesses. Government does not. Everyone knows government is not reason nor representation, it is force. All taxpayers contribute money and the politicians and unelected bureaucrats distribute the spoils among concentrated tiny segments of the total population.

Like I said earlier, don't believe this ignorant immigrant. Ask property owners who have to pay taxes for public schools – even if they have no children. Ask any small business owner - they have more horror stories than I do. What about the owner of an independent fitness center who has to pay taxes so the government can use her money to build a community center with fitness facilities to compete head-to-head with her business? Small business owners have to endure government harassment every single day. Don't believe me? Ask any small business owner.

One annoying explanation for government employees receiving more money and benefits is that they do important and responsible work. That is why strict qualifications are required for government positions. I beg to disagree. Vehemently. As any idiot knows, this ignorant immigrant included, government work, the way it has evolved over many decades, does not require any thinking at all, and hardly anyone has any responsibility for anything. All a government employee ever has to do is look up what the law says. It does not matter if one law is in conflict with another. Just look at the law as it relates to your position. There is no benefit to a government employee's being innovative or creative; better to be a robot. No thinking required. The accepted (though flawed) concept is that everything in the law is correct.

So, back to my original question: why do we need all those qualifications for government workers?

We do not. Yet, government employees are paid as if they make important and momentous decisions! As I've been saying all along, you should not believe this ignorant immigrant. Next time you speak to a government worker, see if you can get them to tell you their job level, what their benefits are, etc. You can then check out the government websites that show salary ranges for various job positions. In this country it is very impolite to ask directly what a person makes. Then, ask them to describe what they do. Now, compare their pay and what they do to yours in the private sector. See if that does not make you gag. Keep in mind that you support all these workers with your taxes. Whether you like it or not.

THE POST OFFICE

Now you got me started. The ignorant immigrant wonders why the post office is given a monopoly? I am told again, it's the law. The Boy Scouts cannot deliver Christmas cards locally as a fundraiser; it's illegal. UPS and FedEx deliver packages and overnight mail – not normal mail. A magazine reported that the USPS could impose fines if employees of a private company hand-carried letters overseas. Also, the USPS claims the right to determine whether messages were sufficiently urgent to warrant overnight delivery. It was reported that the post office once tried to stop the Atlanta Braves from delivering their tickets via UPS. Next time you hand-carry a letter for a relative in LA or NY, or wherever, be really careful – there could be postal inspector waiting to cite you for a federal offense.

Some people say the postal monopoly is defined in the constitution. That's the best way to scare an ignorant immigrant. But even in all my ignorance, I doubt if the U.S. constitution would be that specific. Actually, my research shows the constitution states that the post office shall be "one of the organs of government necessary to provide for the harmony and proper intercourse among states."

As an ignorant immigrant, I cannot imagine how the constitution can be interpreted to have a meaning that results in an unfair advantage towards private business.

Also, I see no mention of making it a monopoly – to the exclusion of all others.

We are told that the post office does not use any taxpayer money at all. I think this is the biggest lie this ignorant immigrant has heard repeated over and over. And, sad to say, many people believe it too. It just ain't so!

While it may be true that the USPS probably (I don't really know) gets no direct cash from the government, it is tax exempt and can borrow from the Treasury. The Postal Service can also borrow money at low government rates that are not available to other entities! Furthermore, the fact is that the post office is exempt from paying many of the taxes and fees that every private business is required by law to pay. No vehicle registration, for example. No real property taxes. No traffic tickets, etc, etc. Beat that!

Private people and businesses are required to pay taxes for vehicles, real property, traffic tickets, etc., and the post office piggy-backs for free and uses the very same services – repeat, for free. Last I heard, Uncle Sam also pays the pension benefits of retired postal workers. That sure sounds like "taking taxpayer money," to me... I may be ignorant, but I'm not stupid.

Meantime, the USPS reports increased productivity in its services like letter delivery. I look at it this way. In the past, carriers would deliver mail to individual mailboxes – imagine the number of stops carriers had to make. Now, with cluster boxes (as many as 16 mailboxes per cluster) the carriers just deliver to the cluster box and they're on their merry way. So, it's true, any fool can see that, with cluster boxes, carriers can deliver more pieces of mail per labor hour. Improved productivity. I am sure the USPS' increased productivity is reported far and wide, to the Postmaster General and several congressional committees, etc.

Yes, that is labor productivity. But what about the investment on the physical facility – the cluster boxes? And what about the labor that was effectively transferred from the carriers to the customers? In effect, the clear increase in labor productivity is offset by a) the increased investment in physical facilities (cluster boxes) and b) the reduction in service (customers now have to go out to the cluster box and pick up their mail). I would like to see the net result of all these factors.

Finally, the post office claims their services are inexpensive; for example, they say $0.39 is really cheap for a first class letter. No one can really know. Again, I look at two aspects that affect the post office's costs and overall efficiency. The good: very large volume due to its monopoly - which can result in possible economies of scale; less expenses due to no taxes, no vehicle fees, no this, no that. The bad: whatever you say, a monopoly makes organizations less inclined to be efficient; an external threat to one's existence is usually the most effective way to compel an organization to be efficient and keep cutting the fat. I bet for the Post Office, the bad outweighs the good.

I really have no idea if $0.41 for a first class letter is cheap. As I said, I can't compare it with any equivalent service. But I want to ask the reader a question: If only one company is legally allowed to make SUV's, how much do you think an SUV would cost ?

Think about it. Then, decide if the $0.41 rate is cheap.

MGA DILANG PILI-PILIPIT (TWISTED TONGUES)

May I humbly propose a way to add a little something to the conventional party repertoire of piñatas, pin-the-tail-on-the-donkey and musical chairs? Here are some tongue twisters I made up that may add fun to your parties or get-togethers. The idea is to ask each guest to read out loud a tongue-twister and see which one gets the biggest laugh.

First get contestants, preferably young (or not so young) people who are not familiar with Tagalog. Next, devise a way of selecting which tongue-twister the contestant should recite out loud. (Dice can be used, or slips of paper with numbers, or playing cards.) Go through the contestants one by one. Oh, by the way, be sure to distribute copies of the tongue-twisters to all other people present. Finally, let the group decide on the top three contestants by acclamation and award them top prizes. You might want to give each contestant a fun little prize for providing entertainment.

1. *Pumili at bumili si Billy ng mga bote na may bituka ng butiki sa botica.* (Billy selected and bought at the drugstore bottles which contained bowels of lizards.)

2. *Bababâ ka ba ? Eh, bababâ rin ako.* (Are you going down? Eh, I'm going down too.)

3. *Pinatong-patong ni Pisto ang pitúmpung-pitóng putíng patíng at tupa.* (Pitso placed on top of one another seventy-seven white sharks and sheep.)

4. *Kapapansiteria mo pa lang, magpapansiteria ka na naman.* (You've just been to a noodle place, and you're going to a noodle place again!?)

5. *Pinaputî ni Tepiterio ang pitóng putíng putong patong patong.* (*Tepiterio* whitened seven white rice cakes that were on top of one another.)

6. *Pag dapo ng bubuyog* (When the bumblebee lands.)

7. *Mukhang dugtóng-dugtóng at dikít-dikít ang mga pagóong kasi tabí-tabí at sunód-sunód.* (The turtles seemed connected and stuck to each other because they were side by side and in sequence.)

8. *Pugong bukid, pugong gubat* (Mountain quail, quail of the jungle.)

9. Kabilugan ng Buwan, Buwan ng Kabilugan

10. *Palakang Kabkab, kumakalabukab, kaka-kalabukab pa lamang, kumakalabukab na naman.*

11. *Aklat Pangkatagalugan* (Tagalog book)

12. *Sinusi ni Susan ang sisidlan ng sisiw.* (Susan locked up the coop of little chicks.)

13. *Notebook at aklat, notebook at aklat, notebook at aklat, ...* (Notebook and book...)

14. *Minimikaniko ni Monico ang makina ng Minica ni Monica.* (Monico repaired the engine of the Minica owned by Monica.)

15. *Ang relo ni Leroy ay nagka luray-luray.* (The watch of Leroy is all worn out.)

16. *Pasko, Paksiw, Pasko, Paksiw, Pasko, Paksiw, ...* (Christmas, Vinegar/Ginger Stew...)

17. *Ako ay biik, ikaw ay baboy!* (I am a baby pig; you are an adult pig.)

Traditional Filipino
Last Names

At some time in the recent past, it seemed to me that there are very few remaining truly Filipino last names. The most common ones I recall are: Kalaw, Batongmalaque, Macapagal, Lagac, Caturay, Katigbak, Mangune. On deeper thought, I found that just among the people I've encountered or heard about, there are a lot with traditional Filipino names.

Social observers say the Filipinos who, during the Spanish regime, were not subjugated for civil control and oppressive taxation, were able to retain their local (traditional) last names. I think these people lived away from the large population centers. People who lived around large towns and cities usually had assigned last names that began with the same letter. Not surprisingly, the assigned names were Spanish. The Bicol town of Oas in Camarines Sur comes to mind; many people had last names that began with "R," like Realuyo, Rodill, Ribaya, Rabaya, etc. If I remember right, around Legaspi City and Daraga in Albay the names began with the letter "M" and "N."

I selected a few traditional Filipino names that I can match with people I remember from childhood, school, work, neighbors, news, etc. I've also added from my memory some names that, to me, sound like traditional Filipino.

If you find here names of people from your nostalgic past, please do not contact this writer for information. I do not want to be involved in contacting your old lovers or people who stole your lover, old classmates, people who owe you money or people *you* owe money, teachers who gave you failing grades, lost relatives, deposed dictators, fugitives who may be hiding weapons of mass destruction, old business partners and the like.

Abao
Abat
Abaya
Ablang
Abueg
Adlawan   The name means "daily," Cebuano.
Agatep   The name means "thatcher," Ilocano.
Agbayani The name means "to be heroic," Ilocano.
Agbulos   The name means "to let go," Ilocano.
Agcaoili   The name means "to hold on to," Ilocano.
Aggabao
Aglipay   The name means "to play w/ lipay seeds," Ilocano.
Aliling
Alindogan   The name means "beauty."
Alunan   The name means "to swamp," Tagalog.
Amaba

Ampon   A top Philippine tennis player in the late 40s, Felicisimo was his first name. This last name means "adopted child," Tagalog.

Amurao

Ancheta In our university, there was a lunch place in the staff housing area, owned by a person with this name.

Andal

Andaya

Angan   A retired military officer I knew.

Angara I believe a former Supreme Court Chief Justice in the Philippines at one time. The name means "beautiful."

Anub

Aoanan   The name means "to deplete," Ilocano.

Aromin

Ayuyao

Bacani

Bacay   A well known name in Cebu.

Bagnol

Baisac   Name of a manufacturer of *jeepneys* – a vehicle converted for public transport from Eisenhower type army jeeps left by the US Army after the second war

Balagtas   The famous person is of course Francisco. The name means "to trail blaze," Tagalog.

Balangue

Balanon

Balcos   A co-worker civil engineer from long ago.

Balgos

Balingit   The name means "to shake," Ilocano.

Baluyut   The name means "woven rice container" in Tagalog.

Banaag   The name means "glimpse" in Tagalog.

Bantilan   I remember this co-worker fellow was a chain smoker.

Bataclan

Batongbacal   The name translates generally to "metallic rock," Tagalog.

Batongmalaque   The name translates to "large rock," Tagalog.

Baylon

Baylosis

Bayót   A well known name in Visayas.

Bohol   A person who tended the yard at an old school had this name. The name means "knot."

Bondoc   The name means "mountain," Tagalog; likely the origin of the word "boondocks."

Bonoan   The name means "wrestling," Tagalog.

Buduan

Bulatao A civil engineering professor from the engineering college way back.

Bumanglag

Bumatay   The name means "to stand up," Ilocano.

Butalid

Cabahug

Cabaluna

Cabangbang

Cabangon   A name from Pangasinan.

Cabatingan   A Cebuano name.

Cabigao

Cabilao

Cabucos

Caguiat

Cajucom   The name translates as "fellow judge," Tagalog.

Calalang

Calica

Calimbas

Caliwara

Canlas

Canoy

Caoili   The name means "fellow admirer," Tagalog.

Capili   The name means "fellow chosen," Tagalog.

Capulong   The name means "fellow organizer," Tagalog.

Capuyan

Caraan

Carandang

Caringal

Carunungan

Catacutan   The name means "scary," Tagalog.

Catindig

Caturay

Cayabyab   The name means "fellow grain thresher," Tagalog.

Conlu

Cudiamat

Culaton

Cunanan

Curameng

Cusi

Cuyugan   I recall this small Kindegarten in Pasay long ago. The name means "to accompany," Kapampangan.

Dacanay

Daclan

Dacumos

Dadap

Dagohoy

Dakay (Dacay)

Dalope   I recall a Tagalog businessman who ran a tailor shop in Cebu in early 60s.

Dalupan

Danao

Danguilan

Dayao

Delasin

Dimaano The name translates roughly as "untouchable," Tagalog.

Dimaculangan   The name translates to "one you can't short/cheat," Tagalog.

Dimagiba The name means "unbreakable/indestructible," Tagalog.

Dimalanta   The name means "tireless or won't wilt," Tagalog.

Dimaporo

Dimasalang

Dimatulac   The name means "can't be pushed," Tagalog.

Dimaya

Dimayuga   The name means "unshakeable," Tagalog.

Diomampo

Duldulao

Dumagat   The name means "to move out to sea," Tagalog.

Dumdum

Dumlao   The name means "be surprised," Ilocano.

Dungca

Gaboya

Gador

Gaffud

Galang   The word means "respect," Tagalog.

Gapasin

Gapud

Gapuz

Gatdula

Gatmaitan

Guinto   The word means "gold," Tagalog.

Gumapas

Halili   The name means "replacement," Tagalog; others say it means "deputy chief."

Icasiano

Ilacad (Ylacad)

Ilagan (Ylagan)

Ilanan (Ylanan)
Ilanga
Ilao   The name means "light," Tagalog.
Jaca
Jacutin
Jalosjos
Jumao-as   Last name of a priest I knew in a mountain community.
Kabayao
Kabigting
Kalaw   The name means large bird, probably "hornbill," Tagalog.
Kangleon
Karingal
Karunungan   The name means "knowledge," Tagalog.
Kasilag
Katigbak   The name means "cohort," Tagalog.
Katindig
Labayen
Lacsamana   (Laxamana)   The   name   means   "many inheritances."
Lagac
Lagahit
Lagasca
Lagdameo
Lagman
Lagmay
Lagumbay   The name of a former senator from the old days.
Lansang
Lansangan
Lapuz
Layug (Layog)
Licuanan
Lomuntad

Lontok (Lontoc)
Lugtu
Lukban, (Lucban)   The word means "grapefruit."
Lumanog
Lumontad
Mañalac   I believe there was a Senator, again in the old days.
Maambong
Mabini
Macabenta
Macadangdang
Macalino
Macalintal
Macapagal   The name means "tiring."
Macapinlac (Makapinlac)
Macapobre
Macaraeg, (makadaig) The name means "winner," Tagalog.
Macaranas   The name means "to experience," Tagalog.
Macasaet   The name means "diligent, hardworking," Ilocano.
Macasero
Macatangay   The name means "one who takes away/grabs," Tagalog.
Macatulad   The name means "imitator."
Madamba   The name means "one who is loud," Tagalog.
Madarang   The name means "to burn," Ilocano.
Magalona   A television celebrity in the old days.
Magbanua   The name means "to go to town."
Magdaluyo
Maglalang
Magpale (Magpali)
Magpantay   The name means "to equalize," Tagalog.
Magpayo   The name means "to advise."
Magsanoc
Magsarili

Magsaysay   The name means "to tell," Tagalog.

Magsino   The name means "to look closely," Tagalog.

Magtanggol   The name means "to defend," Tagalog.

Magtoto   The name means "true to one's word," Tagalog.

Mahinay   The name means "slow," Cebuano.

Maigue   The name means "well, good," Tagalog.

Majul

Makalintal (Macalintal)

Makayan

Malabanan

Malapitan

Malicsi (Maliksi)   The name means "quick, agile."

Malinao   The name means "clear."

Malixi   The name means "speedy," Tagalog.

Mamaril

Mana-ay

Manahan   The name means "to will/bequeath," Tagalog.

Manalang

Manalastas   The name means "investigator."

Manalili

Manalo   The name means "to win," Tagalog.

Manaloto

Mandac

Mandapat

Mangahas   The name means "to be courageous," Tagalog.

Mangaoang

Manglapus

Mangubat   The name means "to fight," Cebuano.

Manlangit   The name means "heavenly."

Manlapaz   The name means "to set free."

Manlapit

Manlongat

Manotok

Mantaring
Maralit   The name means "nobility."
Maramba, (Madamba)
Maranan
Marasigan
Mata   The name means "eye."
Momongan
Munsayac
Musni (Musngi)
Naguiat
Naguit
Nakpil (Nacpil)
Nalundasan
Namoc   The name means "mosquito," Boholano.
Nasino (Nacino)   The name means "take notice," Tagalog.
Nepomuceno
Nicdao
Olalo
Ople
Ouano
Pacana
Pacquiao   The name means "to procure in bulk/wholesale."
Padlan
Pagaduan
Paglinawan   The name means "clear," Cebuano.
Paguio
Pagulayan The name means "vegetable garden."
Palicte
Pamatong
Pambid
Pamintuan   The name means "one at the door."
Panganiban The name means "aware of danger," Tagalog. One of my math professors long ago. How apt.

Pangilinan
Panlasigui   An engineering professor from long ago.
Panuncialman
Pasahol
Pasalo
Patacsil   The name means "deceitful," Tagalog.
Patalinhug (Patalinghug)
Pilapil   The name means "levee/dike," Tagalog.
Pinpin
Poblete
Pumaren
Punongbayan   The name means "town head," Tagalog.
Punsalang (Punsalan, Punzalan)
Purugganan   A former co-worker.
Putong   The name means "crown," Tagalog.
Puyat   The name means "lacking sleep," Tagalog.
Quiaoit
Quilala   The name means "known," Tagalog.
Quiray
Quitain   The name means "to see."
Rabago
Ragasa   A former physics instructor.
Raposas
Saba
Sabile   A former co-worker.
Saguisag   The name means "symbol."
Sahagun
Salonga (Salunga) The name means "in a cave,"
Tagalog.
Sarao   Name of a manufacturer of jeepneys.
Saulog
Sicat   The name means "well-known," Tagalog.
Simbulan
Sisante

Soliman
Sulit   A friend of a former dorm roommate.
Sumabat   The name means "to meet," Ilocano.
Sumalpong
Sumulong   The name means "to proceed forward," Tagalog.
Tablante   The head of some department long ago in college.
Tabo-tabo
Tabura
Tacandong   A co-worker accountant.
Tadena (Tadina)
Tagamolila
Tagarao (Tag-arao?)
Tagle
Tamondong
Tandoc   Our assigned mentor in freshman dorm.
Tapang   The name means "bravery/courage," Tagalog.
Taruc (Taroc)
Tayag
Tiglao
Tinapay   The name means "bread," Tagalog.
Togonon
Tonggol
Tudtud
Tumulak
Ugale (Ugali)   The name means "habit/custom," Tagalog, Ilocano.
Ulanday
Umali   The name means "to smear/stain."
Untalan, (Untaran)
Viray   The name means "large boat," Ilocano.
Yabut (iabut)   The name means "to give," Tagalog.
Yadao

Yambao
Ylacad   The name means "to walk," Tagalog.
Ylagan   The name means "dodge/duck," Tagalog.
Ylanan

DIFFERENT WORDS

The words listed here are but a few of many that have different meanings in different places.

These lines were written to sound like riddles. The reader who is unfamiliar with a word or its meaning or context in a different place may want to bookmark this page and consult with other people. I promise this will be most amusing.

o   Why is *kawat* fun in Bicol but can get you in trouble in Cebu for a crime against property ?
o   Why is it entertaining to *libang* in Manila while in Cebu, it is just a body function – not always pleasurable.
o   A small amount in Bicol won't *dikit* in Manila. But sticky stuff may *pilit* in Cebu without forcing things in Manila.
o   Street corners are *pusod* in Bacolod but in Manila, it's a kind of button close to the belly.
o   In Manila, they do not want *langgam,* but in Cebu, those creatures actually fly!

o Because they're the *ibon* in Manila, which in Pampanga is not quite yet, assuming the egg was fertilized.

o Flying creatures in Manila have *pakpak* but have *pakó* in Cebu, which can't really nail down anything in Manila.

o The *pusa* is a pretty *iring* in Cebu and a friendly *ikus* in Bicol.

o In Cebu, *kamót* can be used to perform a *kámot* in Manila.

o In cold weather, use a *kumot* in Manila but you need to chase the *habol* in Cebu.

o But if you insist on using *kumot* in Cebu – beware, you'll be crumpled.

o It's not violent in Cebu where you *sugat* to meet or come upon people.

o But in Manila, you get a *sugat* only after an actual fight.

o *Sama* in Cebu is a likeness, not always bad - almost like they go together – *samâ* in Manila, but that can also be bad.

o But it's different in Bicol where going together is *iba*!

o The term *asawa* in Manila refers to both spouses but other places use *bana* only for the male.

o If you're sick, take *gamot* in Manila and hope it takes root in Cebu.

o If you still can't follow the story, *magtanong* ka, or juggle the letters a little bit - so you can *mangutana* in Cebu.

o *Salamat* is thankful in Manila but the *mabalus* in Bicol - may sound retaliatory in Cebu because of *balus* (ba-us) Cebu. Then again, it could mean "to reciprocate."

o So take it easy - *hinay-hinay* lang, and you won't be considered *mahina* in Manila.

CHEATING LAS VEGAS

As with any popular place, Las Vegas means different things to different people. Some go for the spectacular and fantastic shows. Others go for the fun of gambling - which by the way is now more elegantly called *gaming*. Still others go for the unlimited dining choices, not the least of which are the all-you-can-eat buffets available all around town. Some people enjoy the endless entertainment and nightlife.5. And, of course, you can also tie (or untie) the knot. There is a wide range of hotel choices from the simplest motel room to the most extravagant and lavish suites – and everything in between.

The dark side of all this glamour is the fact that there are many who try to cheat Las Vegas. By hook or by crook. Constantly. Unceasingly. Each cheater uses different, creative, and sometimes just plain old tricks.

WHO TRIES TO CHEAT THE CASINOS ?

There is such an enormous amount of cash in casinos that bills are not counted individually; they are merely sorted by denomination and weighed. Twenty and a half pounds of $100 bills make up a million dollars. It takes

102 pounds of $20 bills to make a million dollars, while for $5 bills, 408 pounds make a million.

Given the amount of money in casinos, there is more than ample opportunity for cheating by various means. That's why there are the ubiquitous black hemispheres installed in ceilings all over every casino. These are called the "eye in the sky." They contain high definition, real-time digital cameras that are connected to surveillance rooms where security people constantly monitor everything going on inside the casino and its grounds. The digital record of these events is kept for an unspecified period of time – so even an apparently innocent event can later be replayed and analyzed.

There are four employees at the craps table, but if the players are in cahoots, they can still cheat. So each table is watched by a floor supervisor. He, in turn, is watched by the pit boss, who is watched by the assistant shift manager, who is accountable to the shift casino manager. The shift casino manager reports to the casino manager. So everyone watches everyone else. And there's the "eye in the sky." That reminds me of an old saying: The person who is constantly worried that someone may steal from him is often a thief himself.

One account goes that a security guard discovered a mound of $100 chips on hotel grounds, beneath some plants. He reported this to his shift supervisor and was advised to leave it and stand watch behind the shadows. Within half an hour, a dealer who'd just finished her shift showed up and picked up the chips. Surprise!

Another story goes like this. A young kid, barely legal gambling age, with the usual overly casual, almost shabby attire, comes up to the cashier to cash in several chips worth $25,000! It was later discovered that he picked up the chips from the bottom of his mom's purse. The story goes that he was severely disciplined by his parents and was disallowed use of the family Rolls for several weekends. Sorry 'bout that, dude!

They say that as various cheating techniques are discovered, Blackjack table rules change. Some examples: All cards are now dealt face-up. Players can't touch their cards. Only hand signals are allowed. Players can't touch their bet after it's put down. Casinos say that dealers are required to wear aprons to prevent wear on their pants. Maybe so, but they are also required to wear aprons to cover the pockets on their pants so they can't steal chips. Dealers are required to raise their arms, clap their hands and spread their fingers when they leave the table for a break – to show the eye in the sky that their hands are empty. They are supposed to spread out all the chips when paying out a winner just so they don't slip $100 chips under a $5 chip on top of the stack. There is a place for each different chip denomination in racks in front of the dealer; all chips should be in their proper spot at all times – so there can be a spot-count anytime by any manager.

They say the hardest cheaters to catch are the dealers. Some send their buddies pre-arranged code words or body signals unknown to others at the table. In one case, a dealer was in cahoots with a novice player and, without waiting for her hand signals, just dealt cards or moved on, depending on what her cards were showing. Needless to say, she won a lot of money.

Sometimes, dealers steal directly, with aplomb, in plain view of everyone. There was an episode in which a female dealer kept fixing her bra strap when she was actually dropping chips into her cup. She got caught with over $2,000. Another tale goes that a male dealer had an unusual way of fixing his hair while he was really dropping chips into his shirt through the collar behind his neck. Now dealers are not allowed to tuck in shirts or adjust ties. When customers ask dealers if there is any profit-sharing in casinos, one answer would be, "Yes, as long as you don't get caught!"

Of course, it is known that casinos can also cheat, a frequent occurrence in the old days. They would hire special dealers so skillful at dealing that they could ensure a player never won a hand. They could also deal a specific card to any player whenever they wanted.

Even today, perhaps the most obvious way casinos cheat is the illusion they give that you will win, when in fact the mathematical percentages, based on the rules set up for various games, favor the casino. In the nickel slots, the casinos keep about 15-20 percent, the quarter slots 8-12 percent and the dollar slots keep 3-10 percent. Keep in mind, though, that these figures are for the long run.

Of course, the state Gaming Control Board also tries to deter cheating. Every once in a while, they make unannounced visits to a casino, stop the action, collect the dice and put them in marked sealed envelopes for accuracy testing by a laboratory !

CHEATING AS A TEAM SPORT
Another tale goes that a man was wandering aimlessly around the casino blackjack tables with several chips in

his hand. Every once in a while, he would suddenly go to a table, place a couple of bets, take his winnings and leave, only to resume wandering aimlessly around the area. He could not be suspected of counting cards since he only played a few hands. Security quickly deciphered what was going on. He was part of a team and his cohorts were counting cards at a few blackjack tables. When the card count at a particular table looked good, he was signaled to come over and place a bet - just as another cohort would immediately leave a seat for him to take over. The "eye" quickly identified his three partners. They were not immediately apprehended. A casino host approached the winning player with congratulations on his skill and luck and offered him a comp (complimentary) room for the night. Hotel security was alerted to wait about twenty minutes before going up to the free room. Sure enough, within ten minutes, his cohorts were all headed up to his room – obviously to divide up the winnings. There were advised that they were no longer welcome at the casino and that their pictures from the surveillance cameras would be disseminated among all other casinos in town.

Counting cards does not mean remembering all the individual cards that have been drawn. Counting individual cards may be feasible for a single deck game but it becomes unmanageable for a six-deck game. Card counting was developed by Edward O. Thorp, a UCLA mathematics instructor who published a book in 1962. The technique described in his book involves keeping just one number (a running count) in your head. When that running count is +2 or more, odds are in your favor and you are advised to bet high. If the running count is negative, lower your bet. Thorp divided the fifty-two cards in the deck into three groups. Each card counts for either a +1 (2,3,4,5,6) or a 0 (7,8,9) or a –1(10,J,K,Q,A) . You start with a running count of zero for a newly shuffled shoebox. After that, you should take note of the value of each card that is dealt and keep the running count in your head. They say it's that simple. I always wondered.

I don't see it as a simple thing to keep track of each card that is dealt – even if you have to keep track of only one running count. Many people apparently try counting cards but they are quickly identified by the casino shift managers, who are often expert card counters themselves.

A couple was at the craps table placing exactly opposite bets such that when one spouse lost, the other won. It would be a wash, at least most of the time. The slim casino percentage is what assured the casino of a win over the long haul. Meantime, the couple was racking up comp points towards casino freebies for high rollers.

A cheating team player can also place a bet after betting is closed but while the roulette wheel is still spinning. The dealer would quickly pick up the bet and restate that betting is closed. A brief argument ensues. Meantime, another team player places another bet on another part of the table! There are many other types of distractions.

An elderly woman is playing the slots with her large purse by her left side. A person she's never seen before approaches from her right and speaks to her in a soft voice – distracting her and then disappearing. Later, she finds that her purse is gone too! You can be sure these teams have a quick get-away path out of the crowded casino.

A veteran casino shift manager reports that there are skilled craps players who can switch dice without anyone noticing that a loaded dice had been tossed into the game. These con men are advised to leave because their play is "too strong" for the casino.

There is the old trick where people switch a stack of $1 bills for a stack of $100 bills or the other way around, depending on the outcome of the game. The cheater's hand should be quicker than the dealer's eye! You can be sure this player has a partner somewhere trying to distract the dealer.

How Some Try to Launder Money

When someone deposits cash over $10,000 in a bank, the bank is required by law to report the transaction to the government. This is no problem for mom-and-pop groceries that have nothing to hide. However, if one is engaged in an enterprise that is not totally legal and involves a whole lot of cash, one definitely wants to stay below the government radar. Buying some things costing hundreds or even a few thousand dollars in cash may be no problem, but one becomes incredibly conspicuous when buying a $65,000 car with cash! Hence, for people with a lot of paper currency obtained from some nefarious enterprise, there is a need to clean, that is, to "lauder" the money.

Say someone has around $300,000 in cash from a dubious endeavor. One way of laundering it would be to make thirty deposits of $9,999 and hope the bank doesn't catch on. All I'd say is : Good Luck. It becomes very unwieldy when the amount goes higher. Please, if only someone would accept the $300,000 cash and issue a valid check even for a smaller amount, say $250,000. Then, that $250K could be deposited in a bank account and would be clean! Or maybe a business could enter many phony transactions in its books, deposit the cash a little at a time, pay sales taxes on it, pay taxes on the profit, and the leftover "profit" would be legitimate, "clean" money ! There are surely many other ways.

One casino story tells about a man who bought $3,000 in chips and played and lost $50 - then cashed in all his chips and requested a casino check. He then bought more chips for $5,000 and played a little and cashed in. He did this several times until he was approached by the casino shift manager who said he could no longer buy chips unless he actually played. They say he was apparently laundering money. He probably had several hundred thousands in cash and he needed a hotel check to make it clean. His (dirty) cash would now be clean money – not the unwieldy cash that arouses suspicion when used to purchase expensive items like cars or condos.

CASINO CHASERS

It is perhaps not unexpected that some people, seeing all the money available in casinos might be tempted to harass the casino into giving them some of it, by hook or by crook. A large established hotel at the northern end of the Vegas Strip was hit with over twenty thousand claims each year during the late 90s. These claims were filed by angry patrons for various real, imagined or contrived harm. Casinos probably get hit thousands of times a year with one form of claim or another.

One woman claimed she was robbed by some thug inside the casino and demanded immediate cash compensation of $2,000. She showed scratches on her face and bumps on her jaw. A review of the surveillance cameras by casino management showed her injuries were self-inflicted in a corner of the hotel lobby!

Two fellows claimed they slipped on banana and orange peels at the base of an escalator and demanded cash compensation. They had a group of British tourists as their witness. The cameras showed that these two funny guys in fact put the fruit peels on the floor themselves and actually waited for the tourist group to bear witness to their "accident." They were politely advised that filing false claims is against the law.

Some accidents are really just accidents. Usually in real honest situations, the injured person is extremely embarrassed and does not claim anything. In cases like these, casinos often offer a complimentary coupon (for something).

One couple demanded cash compensation from the casino because they claimed someone had deposited a large *something* in the toilet of their room. They reported immediately flushing it. The couple said that nothing of value was stolen from their room – everything was intact: jewelry, gold watch, traveler's checks, etc. The management apologized and moved them to another room. Casino management then reviewed the computer record of all (card-swiped) entries into their room during their stay. All recorded entries were by the couple's cards.

KEEP SMILING!

Always remember, in a casino, each employee has a responsibility and is watched by someone and so on up the chain of command. The friendly tourist you talk to at the lobby may be a plainclothes security person hired by the casino. Everybody watches somebody. And the "eye in the sky" watches everyone. So, as a patron of casinos, you should just keep smiling 'cause you can be sure somewhere you're on television!

Don't Mistake
Schooling for Education
- A NOTE TO THE RECENT GRADUATE...

REALITY AT THE UNIVERSITY

It was spring in the early 2000's when I first accepted a semester teaching appointment at one California State University campus. My designation was Lecturer in Operations Management. All my students were Juniors and Seniors. Since that initial semester, I have been fortunate to have classes of extremely animated and inquisitive learners, and since I teach at night, my classes are inevitably comprised of a mix of working people and full-time students.

Being a part-time lecturer has its benefits. One is being able to present substantial real world examples to illustrate the concepts in the textbook. And also perhaps, I am more credible when compelling the working students to please provide real-life examples from their work to the whole class. I believe that discussing real life situations with textbook theory is priceless. It provides additional education that cannot be taught in the classroom.

It is said that, "anything worth learning at all *cannot* be learned in a classroom." I believe that's a bit harsh. Doubtless, many things can be learned in the classroom, but let us not forget the many things that *can* only be learned *outside* the classroom.

We all know of engineering graduates who have only a vague idea of how a power plant operates or how machine tools run; or of the honors MIS graduate who is unable to deal with co-workers effectively; or of intelligent accounting students who don't know the tax procedures at city hall. That is exactly what I want to point out: Education is composed of more things than just schooling. There is a difference between schooling and education. *Real* education is necessarily a blend of schooling, experience, and real life street smarts.

A College Diploma

In due time, all the students in my class will receive a piece of paper called a diploma. The diploma proclaims their achievement and emphasizes to all "men by these presents" that this achievement (of graduation) bestows on them the "rights, duties and responsibilities thereto appertaining." Nice-sounding words.

Don't get me wrong. A college diploma can have great value. But all my students agree that a diploma without personal effectiveness skills and real work experience gets stale very quickly. The value of a diploma diminishes steeply in the first few years after graduation. My students shudder at the inevitability that a college diploma loses currency long before its owner becomes successful in a business or a job. And surely, a college diploma becomes stale, out-of-date, and possibly sour many years before the college loan has been completely repaid.

That is the reality of college. That is the reality of student loans. That is the reality of life. It is not unlike the certainty of owing more on the (once) new car than it is presently worth.

Fortunately, there are ways around this apparent dilemma.

Personal Effectiveness
It may have surprised the students that we discussed personal effectiveness issues in our class on Operations Management. We talked about how one's future overall success and happiness in life is governed in large part by both technical competence and personal effectiveness.

All of us know people with superior intelligence and unquestioned technical competence who are pitiful failures in their jobs and life. We agreed that we don't have to be like those kinds of people.

I asked my students to imagine the total number of graduates in the football stadium on commencement day. Close your eyes, I said, and picture that mass of graduates for a minute. Then I asked them how they could distinguish themselves from all the other college graduates. Deafening, scary silence.

We discussed that one way to stand out among the crowd of college graduates is to continually develop one's personal effectiveness and find ways to network professionally and socially. Developing oneself basically involves strengthening one's competencies and improving in areas of weaknesses. Some areas for personal development are listed below. Acquiring and developing these skills will enrich your life and complement your technical skills.

1. Personal appearance – Neat personal attire and grooming is noticed, especially in these times of wild dress. Remember the old adage is true: you never get a second chance to make a first impression. A visual first impression certainly goes a long way.

2. Speaking clearly and concisely – Are you comfortable with your speaking skills, can you speak concisely? Do you mumble or rush your speech ? Do you say "Um" or "Uh" every two seconds?

3. Networking – a technique of amplifying your capabilities and finding opportunities. Do you keep in touch with a lot of people? The many available free web-based email service all have capabilities to manage contacts.

4. Presentation skills – Confident oral presentation skills always stand out. Get rid of stage fright. You should actively find opportunities to speak before a group.

5. Math, financial, technological skills – Do not ever be one who routinely says, "I'm not really good at math," or "I'm not really computer-savvy." Personal effectiveness demands that you use available technology tools to enhance your capabilities.

6. Effective team leadership, supervision and organization skills – Always a premium in business and other spheres of life. There are many opportunities everywhere to participate as a team leader or a team member.

7. Negotiation – Every situation has many aspects that can be negotiated. Do not limit negotiation to just price and product features. Observe and learn from car or furniture salespeople.

8. Sports – are you a sports enthusiast of some kind? Remember the saying: "sound mind in a healthy body"

9. Bureaucracy – Knowledge of the intricacies of some form of bureaucracy is always a great personal skill to possess. I don't care what field you decide to pursue, there will be always be a lot of need and opportunity to hone your skills in some form of bureaucracy.

10. Brokering – of whatever kind of service or good. Brokering is the act of being the person in the middle of a transaction. It requires good understanding of human nature since you will be dealing with many people on both sides of the transaction.

11. Research skills – there are many reliable information resources outside the internet.

Of course, there are more.

NETWORKING AFTER GRADUATION
After graduation, a whole new set of disturbing circumstances emerges in the realm of networking. No more

regular class schedules. No more coming to the university everyday. No more meeting classmates regularly or seeing the various bulletin boards filled with announcements. The situation begins to sound a bit scary.

As a recent graduate, you may want to invest in a name card. Yes, the usual business card size. You can print your name, contact and a few words about your job, business or social objective. Cards can be printed conveniently at Kinko's or OfficeMax, or many others. You can also print them yourself. Business card stock can run $15 for 200 pieces. All word processing software should have a ready template to enter your info.

When giving out your card, try to get one in return and put a date on it for your database of contacts. A simple database of contacts can be developed using Excel or Access; I prefer the latter as it seems easier to look up needed data. Actually, the easiest method might be to use the existing contact manager in your email software. Whatever you use, you will want to backup this info periodically.

If you like, you may want to set up a catchy domain name and maintain a basic website for a few dollars a month. If you don't want to spend the money, you can probably maintain (clean it up first) your free student website with your university. Did you even use the free student website space provided by your university? If not, that was an opportunity missed.

You may want to look at these opportunities to network.-

✓   Student associations – often welcome alumni to join activities

✓ University alumni association
✓ Professional societies, student chapter
✓ Civic clubs – many in most big cities
✓ Volunteer opportunities – like SPCA, school PTA, Friends of Library, Community Services, Cancer Society, Diabetes organizations, blood banks, etc.
✓ Ethnic associations – usually have business opportunities with socials
✓ Church groups – can lead to business and social opportunities
✓ Sport associations – little league baseball, swim teams
✓ Your fitness or sports club – wide variety of people
✓ Family gatherings – gather info on relatives from all over

In Conclusion

Was it deceitful that I made a distinction between schooling and education? Not really. Come to think of it, good thing I did. We did not want to continue thinking that schooling is the only (or the biggest part) of education. It would be unfortunate to gain a false sense of security after we graduate – that is, after we finish our schooling. We should not fall in the trap of believing that our education is complete on graduation day, the day we receive a piece of paper called a diploma.

Good thing we were reminded that schooling is only a very small part of education; that there are many other real-world educational opportunities all around us. Education should never stop; it should be a lifelong endeavor.

Good thing we are aware that we need to continually learn more of both *hard* skills (technical) and *soft* skills (people skills, street smarts, real world stuff).

Good thing we know hard skills are easy to obtain through schooling or even self study. Good thing we know soft skills can be hard to get through schooling but can be acquired through many other means.

Good thing we now know that a combination of both is what we all need to make us more effective professionally, socially and in life.

Congratulations to all new graduates!!

COPY WATCHES AT A
BEER HOUSE IN MANDALUYONG

It must have been some twenty years ago. I was on vacation and stayed at a cousin's place in Mandaluyong. I played tennis in the afternoon at the courts near the *municipio* (municipal buildings). After tennis, I usually went to La Tienda, a Spanish-owned grocery store at Burgos in Makati to join some old friends for war stories and a few bottles of San Miguel Pale Pilsen. For some reason, one afternoon, I was unable to go. Instead, I went to a little corner honky-tonk, the equivalent in Manila of the ubiquitous neighborhood taqueria or tavern in many California towns.

Hi, hello to a couple of people I didn't even know. The band was not bad, they were terrible. The servers were not good-looking; but they were definitely rude. The restroom was the usual – you know, stinky. Beer was lukewarm and I had to put ice in it.

Eventually, a fellow who I would later learn was the owner came over to chat with me. He looked like the usual beer house owner, smiling and saying hello to everyone. Please buy the tasty pork barbecue and spend money in my beer house. Please make no trouble.

He then noticed the simple but elegant Omega watch I was wearing. It was a gift from a co-worker a few years back who had bought it in his hometown - Singapore. Yes, in spite of the severe social engineering of Senior Minister and Former Prime Minister Lee Kuan Yew, there are copy watches available in many places in Singapore. It had a simple white-face design, roman numerals, date, quartz – a design that probably was not available from Omega.

The beerhouse owner said that if I was so inclined he could get me any kind of imported name-brand high quality genuine imitation watch at a very good price. He had some in his office if I wanted to look at some. I was not so inclined and I told him so.

Then, as if to enhance his claim that his goods were of genuine imported quality, he exclaimed that Senator So-and-So had just received his shipments a few days ago. He was, in effect, saying, this is the real imported stuff since it is from the shipment of Senator So-and-so – which had just docked. Needless to say, I had no way of verifying his claim.

He didn't realize that whatever little chance he had of selling me copy watches just disappeared. He was not only glorifying and condoning illegal activity but also providing a ready outlet for the contraband of (elected?) public officials. It seemed to me, as far as he was concerned, he is involved in a purely commercial transaction.

I decided that his indifferent approval of corruption is one of the main reasons the social and economic order in the Philippines will remain miserable for the common *tao* for many years to come.

As it was in the beginning, is now and forever. You know the rest.

Printed in the United States
200484BV00002B/31-81/A